Reconnect Your Life

Reconnect Your Life

30 days to rediscover your real self

ALI MOORE

Reconnect Your Life

First published in the United Kingdom in 2019
by Cavalcade Books
www.cavalcadebooks.com

ISBN 978-1-9996213-4-6

Cover design by Tara Goldsmith
www.freerange-design.co.uk

For Kieran, who has been and will always be my inspiration to continue to work to be a better person in the world. One day we shall sit in the Summerlands together; until then you are loved, missed and remembered forever.

Contents

Foreword

I first met Ali back in 2017 when I was a guest on her radio show, and soon after she asked me to speak at one of her fantastic empowerment events. I was very flattered to be part of both opportunities. When I asked her about why she wanted me to take part, she said it was because of my story. And here is the link to me writing this foreword for her fabulous book.

Everything in this book resonates with me, and I know that you as the reader will find it a huge help too and potentially life changing.

You see, when I look at my story there were key moments when life didn't quite deliver what I was hoping it would, and again you will no doubt understand this too. The key is not actually what life gives you; it's so much more about what you do with that, and the fact you have a choice.

For so many of us, one thing we do lose when we face adversity is our sense of self. This then escalates and it can easily send you into a spiral where you feel completely out of control.

For me, when I lost my *Dragons' Den* business 'Truly Madly Baby', whilst on the outside I soldiered on and took action, inside I felt a huge failure and lost so much confidence.

The impact of showing up as if you're ok but feeling like you are dying inside is draining and I literally had no energy for a long time.

If I had this book back then, I would have learnt so much about myself and had a framework and support mechanism to work through. This would have helped me to recover more quickly and put things into perspective, which is critical when you are trying to move forward.

Reconnect Your Life: 30 days to rediscover your real self is essentially a reality check. Daunting, possibly painful emotionally at times, but the fact is you have a choice. You can stay where you are rambling on through life without truly connecting with anything OR you can read this book.

If you want to dare to dream again, connect with who you truly are and really look at what is important to you, then this book is your starting point. From the beginning Ali takes you into her loving care and walks by your side through every chapter.

Reconnection isn't just about connecting to you, but also connecting to everything in your life – your friends, family, the world around you – and deciding how you want to live every day to the full and with happiness.

It's wonderfully easy to read, and with interactive exercises and practical advice, as well as some great mindset work, you will really discover who the real you is again and how you will benefit the most from this wonderful way of wholly reconnecting.

Ali is honest, authentic and a genuinely lovely person. If you never meet her in real life, you will definitely meet her in this book. It's full of her knowledge and personality, and it gives back from start to end.

If you have lost yourself, then never fear … you are about to reconnect on a level like you've never known before.

Thank you, Ali, for the gift of this book.

Jules White
The Entrepreneurs' Sales Coach, *Dragons' Den* winner and author of *Live It, Love It, Sell It*

Acknowledgements

I have a lot of people to thank for their help and support in writing this book. Thanks go to my clients who have given such wonderful stories of Reconnection and to everyone in my network who encouraged me to keep going and have been looking forward to seeing the final product. Here it is, and it would not have been possible without all your support.

Thanks also go to Jules White for writing me a lovely foreword and to Suzan and Lewis at Cavalcade Books. Suzan has supported this project for a long time!

And special thanks go to: my Alfie who has stood by me as I have explored so many new adventures and madcap schemes and always believes I will achieve... Proper!; Megan and Emily — strong women who show what resilience and grit look like and who are truly achieving in their own lives making me so proud every day; and to Alfie Bear — the laughter and joy you bring to my life is unmeasurable.

My Story

My life has changed a lot over the past ten years. Perhaps beyond all recognition. Today I'm an accredited life and business coach, mediator and qualified psychotherapist. I love this work. I'm passionate about empowering women to rediscover and reconnect to who they are and become who they want to be. And in my first year of business I was named Best Business Woman's Best Coach National Finalist and was selected to be lead speaker for the Historic Royal Palaces Feminist Fete 2018 hosted by the Tower of London. Plus I was a finalist again for Year 2! Alongside this, I've continued studying towards a degree with the Open University, hosted my own radio show and recently qualified as a community celebrant. I'm also mum or step-mum to five children with ages ranging from four up to twenty-two. I'm wife to Alfie, with whom I live in a cottage next to our favourite pub, alongside a variety of ducks, rabbits, cats and a very excitable Sprocker[*] called Reggie. But it wasn't always like this.

In 2008 my life was at a low point. Recently bereaved – I had lost my baby boy – the relationship I had been in for

---

[*] For the uninitiated, a Sprocker is a Cocker Spaniel / Springer Spaniel cross

21 years had broken down. These were dark days for me and it was obvious a new direction was needed. I changed everything about myself – my location, my job, my hair, my weight. I trained initially as a life coach. I got promoted. I met my wonderful new husband. Life was starting to be great again. But just as I felt I was meeting all my life challenges – as I call them – and restoring some peace and quiet to my life, the depression I had fought with for many years resurfaced. I had to come to terms with the fact that I needed support for the sake of my mental health. And following a severe flair up of anxiety, I sought therapy. Not only did it change my life, because it gave me the inner peace I so searched for, but also it gave me a direction in which to take my life: to help others overcome the pain and unhappiness I had suffered.

And since 2010 I have continued to train and upskill as a therapist and now work with clients to enable them to find their inner peace – or their Inner Roar! My work is focused on the concept of Reconnection. Reconnection is the key to truly embracing self, gaining positive relationships and unlocking our best possible future. I work with clients to enable them to move on from past events and live the life they choose. Each client I work with is an individual, and I use a combination of techniques to make the support appropriate and create an atmosphere that is effective yet relaxing and comfortable. It isn't a one size fits all. Therapy is a partnership and together we make true change. It's about learning about my clients, their needs and of course their worries and concerns. Sometimes I've found myself and a client in a very traditional therapy space one moment… and then, with their consent, exploring something wider or more spiritual in the next. Sometimes the process is very free-flowing, but the goal is always the same: to reconnect my clients to themselves and enable them to move forward.

I am passionate about unlocking individuals' potential, letting them see the solutions they hold themselves, and opening up new possibilities.

Turning the face-to-face work I do with my clients into a book is therefore not without its challenges – I can't write a different book for each of you, but what I can do is share so many of the experiences that have come up throughout my time as a therapist and coach. In this book I will provide you with information, insights, thoughts you can reflect on and a Reconnection programme that will give you the tools for you to see what is really happening in your world, discover you again and put in place steps to create a future that is aligned with intention and purpose.

No matter how dark the days and how lost you feel, Reconnection is possible. Always.

Introduction

HOW TO GET THE MOST FROM THIS BOOK

This book is about reconnecting your life. Reconnection is the key to truly embracing self, gaining positive relationships with those around you, living in this universe we are blessed to have and unlocking your best possible future.

With Reconnection we look at firstly discovering you again – what is important to you, your values, how you see yourself in your roles in life – then we explore relationships and your interaction in the world, creating healthy boundaries and setting our bar high, before finally putting in place steps to create a future that is aligned with intention and purpose.

The Reconnection programme I present here was originally designed for my personal clients, with whom I would hold coaching sessions to guide them through the process and personally see their progress. I can't do that with you, but what I have done is redesign the programme for this book so that you can work through it by yourself unaided and achieve some amazing results.

And the best bit is that it will only take you 30 days! Yes, in just 30 days you will see significant changes in how you view your world.

Over those 30 days we'll work through the three parts of the Reconnection programme as follows:

- Part One: Reconnecting with yourself
- Part Two: Reconnecting with the world around you
- Part Three: Reconnecting with your future dreams and visions

Using the journal and the activities I've included in this book, you will look at key aspects of your life and you will gain insight into:

1. Your true self – rediscovered
2. Your relationships – redefined
3. Your world – realigned with intention and purpose

So, there's so much to gain from the Reconnection programme presented here, but it will require some effort and engagement for you to get the most from this book. Don't worry, it won't be hard work, it will be rewarding and along the way, to keep you inspired, you'll find quotes and stories from people who have benefited amazingly from finding their Reconnection moment. You will see changes in your overall mindset and you will see progress. The book includes exercises and activities for you to engage with along with, importantly, a 30 day journal that I will ask you to commit to completing every day over the 30 days that you read this book. Because this is a book that is designed to be read in a quite specific way. Firstly, please do carry on reading the next two chapters, which will respectively give you an overview of the Reconnection programme and explain all about journaling, but then when you get to the three parts of the book that are the core of the Reconnection programme I will ask you to take things slowly and to complete the 30 day journal as you work your way through these parts of the book. For these three parts I'm asking you to spend ten days on each of them, reading the words and working through the exercises, at the same time as you complete the journal. That way by the time you reach the end of Part Three you will have completed the 30 day journal.

In other words, to get the most from this book:

- Keep reading the next two chapters that will give you an overview of the Reconnection programme, give you some introductory exercises to think about, and explain how to use the journal pages

- Take ten days to read Part One and complete its exercises, at the same time completing days 1-10 of the journal

- Take ten days to read Part Two and complete its exercises, at the same time completing days 11-20 of the journal

- Take ten days to read Part Three and complete its exercises, at the same time completing days 21-30 of the journal

- And finally, read the book's conclusion

Obviously I can't force you to read the book in this way, but it is the way it is designed to be read and the way I believe you will get the most from it.

Of course, working through this book can't be a replacement for supported therapy if that is what is required. Reconnection and Reconnection therapy are complementary to traditional medicine and normally are approved of by modern health professionals. If at any time while reading this book you are concerned about your mental or physical health, please be sure to consult your GP/family doctor.

Overview

RECONNECTING YOUR LIFE

The need for Reconnection

For me connection is vital in life. We as humans are pack animals. We are meant to have our tribes and build our families.

And today we live in a 24/7 world. We expect to have everything now, no waiting. We are "connected" all the time. Arianna Huffington, founder of Thrive Global and Huffington Post, researched how many times people checked their online presence in a day … and it was over 150 times! I think I've been guilty of doing that myself!

But mental health conditions are on the increase. People no longer have true conversations. We don't phone each other. We don't make time to see people even walk by in the street because we are "plugged in".

How is it possible that in a world in which we are always connected, people are dying from loneliness? And how come all the social media posts of the "wonderful" lives people are living leave us feeling empty?

So now it's got to be not so much about connections – but Reconnections. We have got to start getting back out there, firstly reconnecting with who we are, not the social media Instagram personalities we see but truly embracing what it means to be ourselves – the reconnect with self.

Then we need to start reviewing how we reconnect with those around us. Many people find themselves feeling disappointed with friendships or relationships based on unrealistic expectations. We need to start valuing who we have in our lives: the true friends, and seeing what value people bring to us. We need to appreciate them for the value they actually bring, and accept that that value may be different to what we expected.

Additionally, we need to grasp hold of how we see the world and our place in it. It may seem everyone is leading a perfect glamorous life, but life is what we make of it.

Finally, when we have got clarity on these points we can start to re-evaluate where we are going. Are our goals and dreams and visions in line with our true selves? Are they in line with what we value? Will we be happy with the future we envisage when it comes through? If it comes through… Maybe you'll find you have a goal which you haven't made progress against. It will be time to evaluate why this is. Often, I have clients who think they know exactly where they want to be in the future, only to find they either don't make progress to materialise it or they achieve the future they're looking for and it doesn't feel as they thought it would – in each case, perhaps because it wasn't what they really needed.

It's only when you reconnect with all aspects that you'll see how wonderful life truly can be!

What do therapists mean by "Reconnection"?

What does "Reconnection" mean in therapy? It's a term which explains how emotions and actions are placed together to make sense of past events.

Every time we have an experience, however small or insignificant, we will go through a process of evaluating it, creating a memory and assigning a feeling or an emotion to it. We store this away in our brain for use in future experiences. When such an occasion happens, we can choose to pull on this memory. It's useful to note here that memories are always slightly different from the actual event.

Think about a recent activity, a social occasion or a party… Take a moment to go to that memory. I imagine a great number of you are seeing yourself in the picture. But you didn't see that when it happened in real life, right? You didn't see yourself because you were looking through your own eyes. So that's already a slight change.

Memories take on different forms, based on what was important to us, what we prioritise or value and so on. If they concern something we really value, we may hold them in higher regard and have more clarity on them. On the other hand, items which were not significant to us or our world can often be forgotten altogether. They are still in there within the brain, but we don't recall them unless prompted.

As adults, we base all our future learning on examining what has already happened to us. We subconsciously ask ourselves questions, perhaps like these ones:

1. Have I done this task before? – All or part of it?
2. Have I experienced this person before, if so when?
3. How did my experience MAKE me FEEL?

And most importantly:

How safe and secure do I FEEL right now based on my past experiences?

Because one of our primary functions for the brain is to ensure we stay safe, because it's all about survival.

Now, this all works so beautifully when things are going well. The memory is all attached to the right emotion and it all gets sent just like in the Disney movie (*Inside Out*) to the right place: short term memory, long term memory, the big pit of forgetfulness because we don't need it, or it props up our values and core memories.

We build a database of experiences, we grow, we learn, we create values and we create beliefs, and these help us with all the future stuff life throws at us.

Perfect!

But what happens when things go a little out of sorts? What happens if we experience something which causes us concern, anxiety, stress or fear? Does it all still work how it should? What is the key factor in causing us any problems?

Of course, the answer is in one of a therapist's favourite phrases: "Well, it's complex," but let's keep it straightforward here (because we really want to get on with the Reconnection programme, right?)

The most important point to remember here is that it's the emotion which is the key. The feeling.

As the American poet and civil rights activist Maya Angelou famously said: "I've learned that people will forget what you said, people will forget what you did, but people will never forget how you made them feel."

She was right. They may forget what you said, but they will never forget how you made them feel.

And this is truth!

Emotion is what gives us the deep meaning, but also it can give us lasting challenges.

Let's consider some stages that might follow an upsetting experience. Whilst you read through this have a think about what this means to you.

So, every event has an impact – we've got that. Every event will build on our values and our beliefs, and this in turn will impact and build on our sense of self and the world around us.

So, what if you have an experience that leaves you feeling upset? Now when you remember that event you also remember feeling upset. So, what if you have an experience that leaves you feeling "stupid" (harsh word!) Now when you remember that event you also remember feeling "stupid"… So, imagine you had a few similar events and the feeling of stupid kept popping up? Now you might have a belief that you ARE stupid… This can be even more traumatic if not only did you feel stupid, but someone told you something to uphold that, and maybe they even called you stupid. And if you believe you are stupid, then when future experiences or opportunities come up it might affect how you approach them or whether you even do approach them… and so on. You re-enforce your belief that you don't do things well.

This can then become engrained. So, it changes even more, from "I DON'T do that because I feel stupid," to "I CAN'T do that because I am stupid."

And all of this started from perhaps one single event. We focus on it, we put energy into it, we remind ourselves on a regular basis… and we seek out evidence which re-enforces that belief.

We have impacted our sense of self – how we see ourselves in the world – and created a belief around self-esteem and our view of our confidence.

Yes, it might have been placed there by the words or actions of another human being. However, it is us that has built it up. And harsh as that also sounds, it's also very useful to understand it because it means it is us that can create the change.

Now imagine someone had an experience but the feeling was being scared or anxious or stressed. These feelings may pop up not just when the same experience happens but whenever a similar experience happens, or even when there is only a very slight overlap – like being in any crowds if the original experience happened in a crowded place or in a supermarket because you feel perhaps hemmed in. The feelings then cause more anxiety and we wonder why. We don't clearly understand it is simply a memory of something that happened before, so we get stressed about being stressed… and thus people may have panic attacks, which in turn lead to further panic attacks based mainly on the fear of having a panic attack.

Finally, we have trauma incidents which are so painful that the brain really doesn't want to experience them again. In fact, we may supress the memory altogether, but the emotion is still there. The brain is still searching for are-we-safe-and-secure data and individuals may experience difficult emotions without even knowing why. In these cases, individuals may experience flashbacks and may be diagnosed with a condition called Post Traumatic Stress Disorder (PTSD). In cases like this professional support is needed and can be extremely beneficial. In this book we won't be looking at those types of cases, but it's useful to mention them here as an illustration of how the process can build.

Now, the same processes that we have been talking about apply to happy memories too. But these do not cause trauma and thus the memory and the emotion stay connected. We also tend to notice less the times when a similar experience gives us a happy emotion, and we don't spend a lot of time talking about these occasions. Conversely, it is very common for people to go over difficult times, to keep going back to them and thus fuel that negative emotion. We don't treat happy memories in the same way and certainly we are not encouraged to talk about liking ourselves and feeling good about ourselves. These are points I'll come back to later in the book.

The key is that Reconnection is the piece of work a therapist does to put the emotion back with the event and ensure it is filed away in a helpful not hindering way, retaining the memory and knowing there was an emotion but not experiencing an emotional reaction.

Here in this book we are not going into therapy, but it is good to be mindful of what you believe and think about times when you feel emotional – Do you focus on positive thoughts or do you focus on the negative? Do you say phrases such as, "Well, yes but…" before listing the things that might be challenging? Do you dismiss compliments or positive comments because you feel uncomfortable but could talk at length about what you would love to change about yourself?

Remember that the brain puts energy into what it thinks we need based on what we do. So, if you are thinking negative more than positive, chances are you will notice more negative things and put less energy into positive thoughts.

The journaling we're going to be doing can itself help to re-train the brain to focus on the good things in our life, to bring them to the forefront of the mind. Journaling can help us have perspective and create what is known as a positive mindset.

Reconnection in this format is about starting to be aware of what is going on for you in your life right now, not focused on others, not thinking only of future or past, but looking at what is happening and learning about yourself – why you do what you do.

Three steps for the journey

At this point I want to introduce you to three concepts that are going to be key to your Reconnection journey. They will allow you to explore and discover new viewpoints and see things from a different perspective. They will help you to create space for change. The three steps are:

1. Stop–breathe–be present–be mindful

2. Acceptance – of yourself and others

3. Focus – on your purpose and intention

I'm going to talk a little about each of these in turn before you begin your journaling adventure, which I'll introduce you to in the next chapter. I'll be asking you to keep these concepts in mind and reflect on them as you work through the activities you'll find later in the book and as you do your daily writings.

Also, I share some of my own recovery story in these sections to show how it comes together.

STOP – BREATHE – BE PRESENT – BE MINDFUL

I talk a lot about this within my work. We are so busy, busy in the moment, busy in the crisis, busy being busy… busy talking about our "What If" and our "If Only" worlds that we want to arrive at and live in.

Clients will often come to me and talk about this magical new universe that they believe should have happened, or would happen if only… And my question is always, "Great. Why aren't you in it, then?"

And generally, at that moment we STOP! They look at me and then we often get a list of "Well, if they had…" or "I would be if they hadn't…" or "Well, I should have had the opportunity…" And I say, "Great. And then what?"

And we STOP again! You see, they are wanting me to engage in this hypothetical discussion of things that have already happened, that should have happened differently and the change that might have been made – in a world that doesn't even exist! … plus, it is normally all centred at this point around others.

So, my message is it's time to stop, breathe, be present and be mindful.

Mindfulness and its practice are all about being in the present. It's about bringing your awareness to right now. Because when YOU are in the moment, right now, you suddenly see exactly what is going on around you and see things for exactly what they are.

Think about it. We spend so much time brooding on what has happened (the past) and wishing for something different (the future) and we link it to why we are not happy right now, but that link is just our concept.

Right now is not about past or about future. It's like pressing pause on the cartoon where everyone is running around, or like those scenes where the superhero can stop time for everyone else and then they can make some decisions before starting again.

Being in the now creates the space to think!

So, first STOP and now we need to stay in the now, and this is about breathing. The practice of mindfulness teaches us to just focus on exactly what we are doing in the moment, and in this moment you will be just breathing; that's it. So, you will focus on breath.

You can do this right now. **And I'd recommend setting aside just two minutes of your day, every day, to do the following:**

Sitting mindfulness

- Take a comfortable position either sitting with feet flat on the floor or lying down.

- Close your eyes (if you feel comfortable with that).

- Take a deep breath in through your nose, and then as you exhale through your mouth make it slow and controlled – like blowing through a child's bubble wand.

- Breathe in deeply all the way down to your stomach.

- As you breathe out focus on controlling the out breath making it as long and slow as possible.

- You may notice other thoughts popping into your mind. Simply let them drift away and return your thoughts to your breathing.

Just two minutes of mindfulness helps to rewire your brain and create a more focused approach, reducing anxiety and relieving stress.

A Reconnection moment from me

Several years ago, as I mentioned above, I had come out of my first marriage after many years. Separation and divorce are always complex and full on, and mine came not too long after the loss of our son. In the months that followed I worked hard on making change. I changed my job, my location where I worked, my appearance... I was busy being in the moment and working through my hectic life. I filled every moment and I thought I was healed.

Then a while later when things started to settle – I had met the man who is now my husband and was happy in my job and had good friends, the divorce was just about sorted, and everybody was moving on with their lives – something started to happen.

I noticed that anxiety had crept in. I started to have some irrational thoughts, which came to a head when I stepped out of the house one day to feed my cats and got it into my head that a chimp could have escaped from the safari park a few miles up the road. Yep, you heard me right – a chimp. And I thought that if I let the children walk to school on their own, it would be a bad thing. I put the cats inside and I remember feeling sick. My brain was saying on the one hand, "Woman, you are being ridiculous," but the other part of my brain was saying, "This is real – be afraid!"

Thankfully (and I have told my now-grown-up children this story and seen their looks of total horror as they thought it through) I managed to restrain myself from calling the school to explain why they wouldn't be coming in. The panic subsided, but it didn't go away. The "chimp" started to appear on a regular basis. Driving in my car, I would have to pull over to check the boot. Staying at a hotel where there was a tiling façade in front of the shower, I remember sitting in the bath and needing to get out and check the shower.

I was so frustrated! *Why?* I thought. *Why is this happening now? Everything is settled.* But that was the thing. I had been so busy with life and moving on that I hadn't taken time to heal, to grieve, to accept – we will come to that in a while. And whilst I was in the busy phase my brain couldn't get the message through. But when I started to settle, it spoke up loud and clear.

It was time to STOP, and at that point in my life, my journey through therapy and my discovery of mindfulness began.

It's been a long time since that incident, but I know that stopping for clients is vital, then breathing, then to be able to say that, regardless of what did happen and what might happen, "I am here right now and it's OK right now." When you can see that, only then can you start to think about what the next move on the board might be.

Stopping can also be about moving from focusing on others to focusing on YOU. We'll talk more about this shortly, but it can be about understanding that all those phrases about what other people should have done make no difference. It's YOU that is here right now. It's YOU that creates change.

Here's something to take on board. Stopping can be scary. If you have been fully occupied in being busy because you were avoiding the messages coming through, then it's going to take some adjusting. We are a society which is always on the go. It is not really in our culture to have downtime – even downtime is part of a fully structured and organised day. I have written elsewhere about the fact that when we don't have stress in our lives, we appear to just try and go and find it – because peace and stopping is alien to us.

Be kind to yourself. Don't suddenly try and go for full days even full hours of stopping and thinking in the present. Just start to take note. Write down any thoughts which come into your mind that you may want to explore later. Try stopping for just a few minutes in your mindfulness practice.

And if sitting stopping is something you feel you will struggle with – and I get this – perhaps do as I do and practise your mindfulness with yoga or active mindfulness, maintaining a mindful state of consciousness whilst engaging in everyday activities. When you are walking take note of the walk, of what is around you, what you see, hear, smell and feel. Just start to get connected back to your senses and focus on being in the now.

Once we stop and we breathe, we can embrace being in the present. And when you are in the present, you can do whatever is needed to move forward. Take it one step at a time. And of course, we do this through being mindful.

DAILY MINDFULNESS IDEAS

There are many ways you can incorporate practising mindfulness into your daily routine. So, there is no excuse for saying, "But there's no time!"

Mindful drink making and drink drinking

Take account of every step of creating your first drink in the morning, whether it's the vibrant exotic smell of a hot cup of coffee or the brewing of your first cup of tea.

Watch as the water pours into the cup; notice the steam coming up.

See how the colour of the water changes as the ingredients mix.

Enjoy the sensation of the aroma as it lifts from the cup.

Notice the motion of the liquid as you stir it with your spoon.

Feel the warmth as you place your hands around the cup.

Take a small sip and savour the moment as the taste becomes reality.

Mindful walking

So often I see people walking along with headphones in and with eyes on their devices, totally unaware of what is happening around them. Missing out on the world.

Next time you go for a walk unplug yourself and pay attention!

Feel the pavement under your feet.

Feel the air and the temperature around you – what does it feel like on your face and your skin?

Notice the smell of the air.

See what is happening: who is walking by, what cars and traffic there are, how the trees are moving.

Hear the conversations from passers-by and hear nature.

Living a mindful life is about taking time to focus on what is being done – being truly in the activity. Don't think of mindfulness being about sitting in one position and trying to empty your mind. Mindfulness is not about not thinking; it's about really engaging with what is happening. It is not switching off; it is switching on!

Now, if you're finding it hard to remain focused, here is just one idea why that might be.

Our changing world...

Have you ever noticed that as you spend more time in the digital world, your ability to focus in the real world has started to shorten. I know I have. It became apparent when I went back to university to study. When I was younger I used to be an avid reader. I could spend hours just reading stories and enjoying the concentration it brought. It soothed my mind. So, I wasn't too concerned about the prospect of all the reading I would need to do for my degree, the amount of theory I would need to digest. However, I quickly noticed I was constantly distracted – by the small rectangular object that is my constant companion. Just a few minutes would go by before I felt compelled to check it.

Added to this, I would start to read a chapter and find myself struggling to stay in the moment.

We are living in a fog in the modern world, consumed by checking for small bits of information and finding it difficult to focus on activities for any length of time. The brain quickly re-adjusts to what it believes is the norm. And if the norm is to scan items briefly and move onto the next, it will become adept at doing this. But it must make room for this learning, so it will become less adept at long-term concentration. Studies have seen this change of behaviour in our younger generations, who have been in the digital world from a very early age. It is literally changing the way we are digesting information – impacting attention span, ability to focus and memory retention.

So, just like going to the gym and training those muscles to build stamina, you need to start building up your brain muscle. And mindfulness is a great workout.

No longer allowing your mind to wander around aimlessly thinking random thoughts – or sometimes going feral and misbehaving (negative thoughts, anxiety, panic) – mindfulness makes it work. The mental health benefits are clear and just two minutes a day can see you noticing a positive improvement.

Just like we mentioned at the start, disconnect yourself… and get reconnected – with the real world!

ACCEPTANCE – OF YOURSELF AND OTHERS

So, this is a big one: acceptance of self and acceptance of others in our lives. In Part Two later we'll look at expectations we place on people around us and whether these match what they bring into our lives – and whether we can ever, or should ever, look to them to meet our expectations, or if we should accept them for the gifts they do bring. And yes I know, sometimes this isn't what we really want.

But first let's look at the concept of acceptance in our own lives here.

Once you have stopped you will start to review where you are. The first part of acceptance is that you are exactly where you are now. Sure, it's based on your choices and the path you have taken in the previous years, and the past is relevant on your journey, but right now you are where you are – it is what it is.

So, you need to step away from thinking about what you could have been, could have done, should have done and start to look around you right now.

This is important because when we are fixated on either the past or the future, we lose our ability to have true choice.

Perhaps something in the past happened which you really didn't like or was awful. By continuing to bring this into the now, you are creating choice – but it's choice still based on that unlikeable or awful thing or person. So where is your personal power in that? It's back there with the thing or the person, still dictating what you should be doing even now here in the moment.

And that will take those things' power right into your future – and your future will be based on your past events. You need to bring that power back to you, and the way to do that is to stop reliving what has happened and start being right now.

Two ways to tell a story (Owning your power)

Owning your power is how you tell your story. Have you noticed that there are some people who are always bringing up the past? Always talking about how awful such and such a person was? Always talking about how hard done by them they were? Or perhaps you have experienced something awful and there are those people around you who just keep bringing it back up – going over all the gory details. That's one way to tell a story… keeping it in the drama.

That's wonderful for TV and books – but not so wonderful for mental health. It keeps fuelling negative emotions and creates a feeling of being stuck.

I am not saying don't tell your story, as it's part of who you are – or that you shouldn't listen to others tell theirs, because it's part of them too – but tell your story in a way that puts you in the driving seat. Focus on what you have achieved since, look to see the gains and where you are now. Tell your story to help others understand they are not alone in experiences (as many people, and I myself, have done in this book). If people around you try and bring up all the drama, you can just be firm and state that you don't want to go over old ground.

So, acceptance is key: I am here right now – it is what it is. Am I saying sit down, give up? NO!! Now is the time to create new choice from this moment on. The journaling you are about to do on a daily basis is all about looking at what is happening now and what has happened today for you, with you, about you. It's looking for your positive points, your achievements. You won't see those clearly if you are still holding on to everything from the past.

Clients come to me and I ask them to tell me about what they achieved, what they saw. But what often happens is they start on this topic and within just a few sentences they are talking about what they didn't achieve and what didn't happen… and they give me a host of reasons why that was the case.

And you guessed it. I say, "…and what? – The question was what DID you achieve? What DID you see?"

The future you are creating does NOT have to be based on the past. You can make change – right here in this moment.

Now, I appreciate that some of this will mean acceptance of others, but I would suggest you start with self – your life right now. Later in Part Two we will look at acceptance of others in a lot more detail and you will have some great activities to help you work through that.

For now, I want to get you thinking about what you accept and do this in the form of affirmations. These are statements that help you to tell the universe who you are. Use the template below to create three affirmations that you can say out loud to yourself every morning.

For example, one of your affirmations could be: "I accept I cannot change what has already happened."

You will notice the more you do this, the more it creates a powerful feeling within you, perhaps one of calmness, a feeling of being ready.

I accept I ………………………………………………………..

I accept I ………………………………………………………..

I accept I ………………………………………………………..

After my grief, I spent a lot of time thinking *What if...? – What if I had made different decisions?* and so on. This wasn't helpful. It took someone to say, "Do you love your life right now?"

And, I did. That felt quite disloyal, but it was the truth. Then they said, "Well, if you went back in time and changed things, you wouldn't have what you have now. What will you give up?" Then I realised I didn't want to give anything up. And it helped me accept what had been.

That's harder if you are struggling with your life in the present. However, the same format applies – things are now as they are. You can't change what has happened, but you can change going forward. In Part Three we are going to get you working on what you want and what changes are needed.

For now, working together with the first step – Stop, Breathe, Be Present, Be Mindful – alongside practising acceptance, you can start to create new choices – healthy choices, choices which start to define a life that is fulfilling.

- Accept what has happened.
- Accept it cannot be changed
- Accept where you are
- Accept YOU have choice

It's hard to let go

Acceptance can feel like you must let go of things as well. This can feel difficult. A good phrase to think about using instead is "moving forward", as someone once said to me, it's hard to move on – that can feel like just leaving everyone and everything in the past – but moving forward that felt more natural.

In the same way, rather than feeling you need to let go of situations or people – if that feels a step to far or too big to start with – perhaps think about simply letting them be. Just let it sit; let it settle. Small steps.

In Part Two we will also look at the concept of forgiveness and how this is different yet part of acceptance.

FOCUS – ON YOUR PURPOSE AND INTENTION

Once again, this is a concept that came to me by listening to how clients wanted to get on with things. "Goal setting" has become a bit of a buzzword and I have had clients come in with large lists of goals – looking for ways to achieve them and looking for reasons why they are not achieving them, procrastinating and feeling frustrated.

I realised that the goal was designed based on that future we mentioned that didn't exist. The goal appeared to often have no link to what the client valued or what was important. Therefore, it seemed no surprise that little or no progress had been made. It was often based on the wonderful word of "should" – more on that to come.

So, it was time to get aligned – to, of course, get reconnected.

Think of it this way. The external goal is just an abstract. It's needed as it gives you a direction and clarity on the task. But it can be anything and it can turn out to be unrelated to what is needed in your life.

Clients jump to this a lot in the coaching and therapy space, making great lists of "To Do"s but yet again wondering why they (To) Don't! This is driven by a need to be in the busy, in the doing – it is nothing to do with in the being, which is about who you are and how you truly want to be as a person.

So, your *purpose* is that inner goal – it's different. It's what drives you, gets you up in the morning, makes you feel alive. We don't always know what it is; people might search for it, talk about looking for it, etc.

Your purpose, I believe, is always there to discover, and sometimes you are not in that place in your life where it becomes clear. But you know when you've got it – it's that Reconnection moment. You just get it!

Often when we are working at odds with our purpose it creates blockers, so we procrastinate and we question. So, if your goals are not in line with your true purpose, then you put them off … because your true self knows they are not your path to take.

When you understand what your purpose is, and you can embrace that, then you see which parts of your life fit.

Finally, *intention* is the step of how you want to bring out that purpose: your actions or your being.

Gary Zukav, author of *The Seat of the Soul*, states that when the behaviour is congruent with what the soul wants to bring forth, then there is peace.

When you act with the intention that is linked to your purpose, things start to fall into place.

This is when I see clients at a transformation point in their life – there is change coming. They can feel it is needed, but they can't describe it. Something is telling them, "You are not aligned with your purpose, but when that happens your behaviours might be in line with your intentions."

A Reconnection moment from me

I felt this when it was time to leave my corporate life. It was a good company. I was well paid, and I had done very well to reach a senior position. But as the months went on it didn't seem to fit. I felt out of sorts with what I was doing. I was frustrated with how the company worked. But they worked how they worked and I knew that. Then I went on maternity leave.

At this point I had an idea that I wanted to set up my own business. I was now happily remarried, and my girls were grown. Therefore, just as we became independent to travel the world, so we decided to have a child of our own! (I do have to add how funny it was that so many people thought he was an "accident", but no, even at my old age of 40, he was very much planned!)

I decided I would set up my business whilst I was off. However, my little boy wasn't too well in those first few months, and aside from naming my company and registering to get letters from the tax office, nothing else happened. I went back to my corporate life and thought after 12 months off I would be refreshed. But no, even more, I felt this wasn't where I was meant to be. I wasn't doing the work I was here to do. And that nags at you!

So, I left again, thinking I would take a smaller role in another company and then work on my business on the side. However, I am an overachiever, so I just put all my energy into my new role for my new company, who were lovely, but I ended up working full time as before – just for a lot less money. *Still* I was not listening to the message that I was hearing – I was a typical ostrich, head in the sand.

Finally, I made the break. What got me to that point I can't really say. It should have been, oh there is the message and off I go, but I know I stayed until I was disgruntled and miserable… until there was no option left. If only I had listened sooner. But it did happen, and scary as it was I knew instantly it was heading me in the right direction. Now, it wasn't plain sailing as I went on this journey – and I'll share another Reconnection moment later with you about that – but suddenly I had my internal goal, my purpose. I was on track. I was clear on my intention and my behaviour became linked – the resignation, the focus on the business – the Reconnection moment!

As we work through the journaling parts below, we'll look at first removing those preconceived ideas of where you want to go. We'll step away from that imaginary future (as in *it isn't here*) and we'll refocus on how we fit into our world and the relationships around us.

We might then uncover some truths about what is fitting in our lives and what isn't – but now you can ask yourself:

What is not aligned with my purpose and intention?

Why do I behave that way and then not feel fulfilled with that behaviour?

UNDERTAKING YOUR
Journal Journey

So, we've begun thinking about some important questions and have covered a lot of theory; it's now time to put it fully into practice.

Like many people I am an avid buyer of planners, goal-setting diaries and journals, but also like many people I make a great start and then it fades off as life takes over and the year progresses!

However, I also know that journaling as a form of self-awareness is a fabulous tool and can have amazing effects on the mindset we have. So, I'm asking here for you to make a commitment to completing a journal using the pages you'll find at the back of this book for just 30 days – during which 30 days you'll be working through the three parts of the book you're about to get to.

These are the three parts we described earlier:

- Part One: Reconnecting with yourself
- Part Two: Reconnecting with the world around you
- Part Three: Reconnecting with your future dreams and visions

In each part you'll find questions, exercises and reading. As you work through these, you'll see the links to the three steps we've just been talking about:

1. Stop–breathe–be present–be mindful
2. Acceptance – of yourself and others
3. Focus – on your purpose and intention

You'll find longer explanations and some wonderful stories of Reconnection throughout the three parts, but why not also see if you can spot which activities help you to combine the three steps with the different Reconnection stages.

Please don't rush any of this. The activities you'll find in the three parts are designed to be taken slowly to give you time to reflect, review and make notes.

My suggestion is that you take 10 days to complete and reflect on Part One, remembering to fill in a journal page every day as you do so, then take 10 days to complete and reflect on Part Two, again completing a journal page every day as you go along, and finally ten days to complete Part Three, again completing a journal page every day to complete the 30 days journaling.

The journal is based on the one I use with my clients undertaking the Bemoore Reconnection Programme. It's been designed in a style that would keep my busy mind focused and be able to complete what I started!

Each journal page – one for each of the 30 days – has five sections:

1. *My positives*

2. *My top achievement of the day*

3. *Reconnecting with me*

4. *Mindful moment*

5. *Connections I've made*

To explain these sections in turn:

My positives

Here's where you can process your positives. Often we are so busy we miss what's going on in our everyday lives. We miss the small things which actually are wonderful to experience. At the end of each day find 10 things which have been positive in your day. They can be small – in fact small is better. Recognise all the little things that helped you have a fabulous day. Finding your positives every day helps your brain to see what's going on around you. It helps you to see that you don't need big highs (and crashing lows). You have many wonderful events every day.

My top achievement of the day

Each day make a note of the best achievement you had. Following on from the theme that it is the small things which matter, this doesn't have to be a big thing. Sometimes it could be just getting up and showing up! We all achieve something each day and focusing on the thing that you are most proud of – maybe something ticked off that list which is now done or that made you think, *Yes! I did it* – is a great feeling.

Reconnecting with me

When you don't value time for yourself you cannot truly value time for others. What will you do each day to ensure that you look after you? But, now let's be clear – me time is not bath time! It can be, but if the only time you actually have had time to yourself is when you take a wash, you need to look a little deeper. Having time to cherish self and reconnect with self is so important. Yet these are the first things which go out of the window when life takes hold. So always think about taking even 10 minutes a day just to do something for *you*.

Mindful moment

Being mindful is all about being in the present, actually looking around you whilst you walk the dog or go to the shops, seeing what is happening, engaging your senses. Make a note of something that caught your attention whilst you were embracing mindfulness. Did you read a great article? Did you see something that was different? Or did you notice something you want to go back to? This kind of list means you capture those items which have sparked your imagination and helps to create a choice of things to go back to when you need future inspiration.

Connections I've made

This is the one I feel so strongly about. This is about recognising three moments in every day when you make contact with someone else, in person! – not on social media, not virtually but actually connecting. It could be talking to the lady in the shop or smiling at a stranger in the street or on the way to work. Take your headphones off, look up from your smartphone and actually engage with the world around you.

When to do your journaling

You should aim to do your journaling last thing at night. When we sleep the brain will process all the thoughts we have had during the day, making sense of it and filing it all away, including both actions and emotions. By ending your day by reflecting on positive thoughts you are creating a state of mind that is aimed at a positive outlook. You are encouraging positive endorphins to be released. These can aid restful sleep but also start to program your brain to look for more positives going forward.

Also, I am a big fan of actually writing by hand

Some people say, "Well, I can keep all of this on my phone," but I strongly recommend you take the trouble to complete the journal (and the exercises you'll find in this book) by physically writing your answers. You might want to pop a note on your phone during the day to remind you of a Reconnection moment, but then use the art of writing to transfer that into the journal pages of this book. This helps embed these positive thoughts into our mind.

Part One

RECONNECTING WITH YOURSELF

Your initial review

Let's get started on Part One by taking the time to reflect on where you are now.

In this section we look at how you see the world now, where you want to go and what you are currently wanting to focus on. This will help us as we come to review ongoing progress through the 30 day process. There are no right or wrong answers here. Just try to note what is going on for you at this present time.

1. What drew you to the Reconnection programme?

....

2. What three things would you like to focus on during this time?

A. ....

B. ....

C. ....

3. If you could change one thing about your life schedule, what would it be?

....

4. How comfortable are you in being yourself? You can use this scale to help you:

0 _____ 10

Not at all comfortable   Totally comfortable

5. What would you say is your "big goal"? – Where would you like to be moving forward to?

....

6. Where do you see yourself in one year, three years' and five years' time?

....

....

....

7. When you look at your life overall how satisfied are you with where you are now?

. . . .

8. How will you know you are satisfied?

. . . .

9. Describe a future self currently you feel is based on your intention and purpose?

. . . .

. . . .

Your commitment – write down your commitment to completing the 30 day journal in this book. Make it a real goal for you to complete.

I commit to completing this journal journey because / for

. . . .

. . . .

. . . .

Reconnecting with yourself

And we are off! For once, it's all about you, reconnecting with yourself. However, looking at self can feel like an unusual thing to be doing. Although many of us see things just from our point of view, we don't often stop to reflect on what that means. We don't think through what's important to us, what drives us, and how we feel about our roles in our lives.

As you work through this section remember our three steps:

- **Stop–breathe–be present–be mindful** – practise your mindfulness breathing

- **Acceptance** – this is what is happening now in your life, where you are now, but you can make change

- **Purpose and intention** – change will work best when you are centred on your purpose and in line with your intention

Be honest with yourself. Make a note of things which come to mind and don't rush through trying to complete every exercise straightaway. I recommend just doing one a day at most to be honest, to allow time for you to process and reflect.

And remember once you start doing these to also start completing your 30 day journal. The more you learn the more you will gain, and the two parts will support each other.

A review of self

In this section we look at:

- How you spend your time

- What you want to be focusing on

- What is important to you in beliefs and values

- What you *do* focus on

- Your interaction in the digital world

- Your skills abilities and traits to harness

You will learn mindfulness techniques around grounding yourself and being aware of your own emotions.

It is rare to stop and consider who we are, what we bring to the table.

Values

In this first exercise we're going to explore your values, the rules you choose to live by, the things most important to you. When our values are being respected and in place in the environment around us we feel a sense of fulfilment.

When you can highlight experiences which have created that feeling you can start to explore what generated it – so you can recreate it from within.

Step 1: Identify the times when you were most fulfilled and satisfied – use both work and personal experiences

What needs or desires were fulfilled?

How and why did these experiences give meaning to your life?

What factors contributed to your feelings of fulfilment?

Step 2: Based on what created a feeling of fulfilment, where do you see this in your day-to-day life now?

How can you influence this feeling on an ongoing basis?

[ ]

Step 3: Identify your top values

Using the suggested values list below (for reference only as you may have some more which are not listed), and some small sticky note papers if you like, write out your top 10 values. Think about why they're important to you and what purpose they serve in your life. Then complete your answers in the grid below on page 53.

Accountability	Accuracy
Achievement	Adventurousness
Altruism	Ambition
Assertiveness	Balance
Being the best	Belonging
Boldness	Calmness
Carefulness	Challenge
Cheerfulness	Clear-mindedness
Commitment	Community

Compassion

Consistency

Continuous improvement

Control

Correctness

Creativity

Decisiveness

Determination

Discretion

Effectiveness

Empathy

Enthusiasm

Even-handedness

Excitement

Exploration

Fairness

Family-orientation

Focus

Fun

Goodness

Growth

Hard work

Helping society

Honour

Independence

Inner harmony

Insightfulness

Intuition

Justice

Legacy

Competitiveness

Contentment

Contribution

Cooperation

Courtesy

Curiosity

Dependability

Discipline

Diversity

Efficiency

Enjoyment

Equality

Excellence

Expertise

Expressiveness

Faith

Fitness

Freedom

Generosity

Grace

Happiness

Health

Honesty

Humility

Ingenuity

Inquisitiveness

Intelligence

Joy

Leadership

Love

Loyalty

Mastery

Openness

Originality

Positivity

Preparedness

Prudence

Reliability

Restraint

Security

Self-control

Self-reliance

Serenity

Simplicity

Spontaneity

Strategic

Structure

Support

Thankfulness

Thoughtfulness

Tolerance

Trustworthiness

Understanding

Unity

Vision

Making a difference

Obedience

Order

Perfection

Practicality

Professionalism

Quality-orientation

Resourcefulness

Results-oriented

Self-actualisation

Selflessness

Sensitivity

Service

Soundness

Stability

Strength

Success

Teamwork

Thoroughness

Timeliness

Traditionalism

Truth-seeking

Uniqueness

Usefulness

Vitality

Value	Why is it important?	What purpose does it serve in your life?

Now, I want you to cut those values down, very quickly. Remove those which are least important to you as follows:

- In just 30 seconds, remove two.

- Again in 30 seconds, remove another two.

- And finally, another three.

- You now have three values left.

Question:

What do these three values mean to you now?

....

....

How our values are based is so important to understand. They are created at a very early age and are a true reflection of the nature-nurture development cycle. We often don't even know what our values are until later in life when we have experiences that either are aligned with our values or push against them.

I love the analogy of an anchor in the seabed representing those deep-rooted values. All around the anchor on the chain are different values and beliefs. Every day the buoy attached to the end of the anchor is able to bob about on the water, interacting with different values, interacting with different people's ways of doing things. But some of these values are much further away and the chain becomes stretched… it becomes tight… Think about a time when someone was acting in a way which went against your values. It feels like that. You feel stretched, you feel a tightness and it's uncomfortable. Bringing yourself back to your anchor point, your value space, relieves the tension, and so it is in real life.

Now we have discovered what values are important to you, let's look at how you see yourself.

In these next two exercises you will take a look at your true self, what you see and what you like about yourself – what you know to be true.

My "Gingerbread Person"

Too often we think of all the negatives or we play down our strengths. But when we face challenges in life with our true selves and in conjunction with knowing our values, we can make real change.

The "Gingerbread Person" on the next page represents you and you are going to fill it with all the parts of you that make you unique: behaviours, skills, descriptors. However, there is a rule. You must only put in there what you consider are positives or strengths.

When did you last stop and think about what great skills you have, about what you bring to the table?

Being asked to complete the Gingerbread Person has often caused people to actually stop and say, "I can't think of anything." But interestingly, if I were to ask many individuals what they didn't like or what they would love to change about themselves, they would need a bigger sheet of paper!

But this is about your positives. If it helps, think about how your friends and family might describe you. Think about what skills you use on a regular basis, think about how you like to be as a person.

Make your Gingerbread Person as colourful as you like. I recommend you draw it out on a separate piece of paper and then keep this somewhere visible where you will see it every day. The more you notice positive things about yourself the more you will continue to see them, so add to it and build up a picture which celebrates all the wonderfulness that you are.

Client Reconnection story

Maria came to see me suffering from severe anxiety and low self-esteem. She didn't see her worth and would often make negative comments about herself. Although she had friends, Maria would often say they must not think much of her – they just put up with her. Maria had no evidence of this and yet was so focused on her lack of ability that at every turn in the conversation Maria would put in what she could not do and what she did not do well and how she could do something better.

When I asked her to write down some descriptors of what she liked about herself, she could not think of a single thing. Sentences would start with, "Well, I would like to be… but I am not," and Maria became very emotional.

We took some really small steps forward. We talked about how Maria would like to be; then we talked about why. We started to explore what her friends might see as her skills and what they might ask for from her, at this time avoiding all use of liking self or not liking. We got some words on paper. By doing this, Maria could look at the skills and state whether this was something she liked about herself. From this point on there could be a shift.

Often when people talk about how they want to be, it is because that person is already there inside. What they are really saying is, "I wish I could be the person I am inside. I wish I could embrace that and let that person shine."

So, if you are having some challenges with this exercise, I hope you can revisit it and find that one thing that can be the catalyst to liking yourself.

"I look in the mirror and love what I see"

Picture yourself looking in your mirror – you are in a wonderful outfit; you are feeling amazing.

Write down all the statements that come to your mind as you look at yourself and truly appreciate what you love about the person you are and how you look.

Doing this from a visualisation point of view can be easier for some people than facing their own reflection in a physical mirror.

Whatever you notice, write this also on your Gingerbread Person page. Add in any traits you find come into your mind and write down what you notice about your physical appearance that you liked – just one small thing can be the start, perhaps the colour of your eyes is a safe place to start or your hair.

All the time we are doing this, we are retraining our brain to notice positive things about ourselves – changing the energy flow from going straight to the negative, and beginning to see ourselves in a new light.

So, there may be things about yourself that you do want to be different; if that's the case, it is better to approach these with an overall positive mindset – enjoying what makes you you.

Some great questions to ask yourself about changing your body image are?

1. What is my purpose for wanting to change? – Note here if it is positive or negative focused.

2. What will be different after the change?

3. Is it something I can influence?

4. Is it healthy to want to change this?

Here's an example.

You may be aware that you are heavier than you would like to be.

An unhealthy approach would be to want to be slimmer or reach a certain weight goal, and in order to do this you would reduce your meal intakes and deny yourself different foods.

A healthy approach to change in this instance is to want to create a healthier and fitter body, not to focus on weight loss or size. You can certainly influence this by getting some good advice on exercise and nutrition and making modifications to your lifestyle.

In the first instance it is all about your overall image and it's maintained by rules. In the second it is all about self-care and support.

It's also great to look at how our body came to be as it is.

Who did you inherit certain features from? Perhaps facial features from your parents, your curly hair from your nan? Seeing your body as part of your heritage can give a very different viewpoint to how you perceive it – understanding that there is a reason for the way you look and that it connects you to your family and your history.

Have a look through old photographs, if that is possible, and start to compare your features to those of your family, building up that picture of Reconnection.

Please note that I understand for some readers this will not be possible. Perhaps you have no record of your past family; perhaps you are in an adopted family. Only do this exercise if you feel comfortable carrying it out. And if not, you may find the next approach better suits you.

We focus on our body as our self-image – how it looks often in clothes and, of course, back to that mirror image. But let's remember that our bodies are all about practicality. We are designed in this way to best work within our environment, and even if we have physical disabilities or differences to those around us, our body is amazing at adapting to work in the given environment.

So, it is also important and gives more clarity that we view our body with purpose. What has your body done for you and allowed you to be over the years? Respecting the work that our body has to do also gives a different viewpoint on how we see it.

Learning to respect our body and treat it kindly rather than simply picking out bits we wish were different is a healthier approach to self-image.

Laura Phelan, Eating Disorder Specialist Therapist and the founder of Phelan Well of Harley Street, has these words to say to help you with your overall positive body image.

Body image is the subjective sense we have of our exterior appearance and our body. Unlike what others see when they look at us, our body image is often different from the objective and actual size and shape of our bodies.

Whilst it is true that both men and women can feel dissatisfied with their body and its parts, there are reportedly more women than men report consistently disliking their bodies. Up to 10 million women in this country who feel depressed about how they look in fact. The emphasis on a women's experience isn't to suggest that body image problems among men are less important than among women, but they are less common and thus less reported. What's more, is that children mostly around the age of 10 are more afraid of getting fat than a parent getting cancer. 47% of girls aged between 11-14 refusing to take part in activities that might show off their bodies in any way. Therefore, negative body image often begins when people are young and extends far into adulthood with these figures raising every day.

So, what can we do to tackle all of this?

Change the conversation, whether you are a loved one, mother, sister, father, partner or teacher. Take the focus off the physical appearance and start complimenting your loved ones for what personal attributes they have, their kind nature of funny story telling.

Spend less time focusing on the media which shows a lot of photo-shopped images and if you do find yourself being impacted, make sure you are aware of the effect of Photoshop, filtering and other ways in which images are manipulated to skew reality, that way you can remind yourself it's unrealistic because it isn't real!

Surround yourself with people who promote a positive self-image, who don't constantly put you or others down based on what they look like.

Encourage and work to develop positive relationships with food and exercise, balanced eating not restrictive dieting and moving the body for health and mental wellbeing.

Overall, having a more positive body image isn't about loving what you see in the mirror and having to be overtly body confident. The first steps are to be more accepting about the body you have, recognising all it can do for you and how it keeps you alive. Body neutrality and body image flexibility are both great to strive for as this is about looking at the bigger picture, and focusing on other things in your life that are more important than your body and physical appearance, start by making a list of 8 things or more that are more important to you.

Finally, at the end of it all when you pass from this world, ask yourself, do you really think people are going to be remembering you for what you looked like?

Client Reconnection story

Tina was the mother of five children all under the age of 10. She had been pregnant or breastfeeding for most of the last 10 years. She was unhappy with how her body looked and often compared herself to her pre-children image. Looking in the mirror, Tina was instantly drawn to the parts of her body she "disliked".

However, our discussion brought out the fact that Tina had actually loved being pregnant and enjoyed the process of feeding her children. This was now coming to an end. Whilst it was ongoing, she hadn't paid much attention to her body – it had purpose. With that purpose closing, Tina was now aware of how much her body had changed. The transition in her role as a mum was a big step for her. It meant a big change in her lifestyle.

Seeing her body for the amazing thing it was – for being the carrier of her children and allowing her to have that closeness to her children for so long – allowed Tina to start appreciating it in its true sense.

Just as she as a person would not go back to her pre-children persona, her body would also not go back to her pre-children days. However, what we found was the pride she felt in herself for being a mother and she was able to start transferring that pride to her body. Sure, Tina wanted to help her body to recover and wanted to have self-care, and with no breastfeeding there was a whole new wardrobe possibility which was exciting in itself. But now Tina was enjoying the process of regaining not her physical self but regaining a part of *herself* – discovering who she was in the new transition of her life.

A Reconnection moment from me

I am a curvy girl. I have fought against this for a lot of my life and it's only now in my 40s that I have started to embrace my body shape. As a teenager I was bullied at school and my defence for this was to restrict what I ate to the point that I needed to see a dietician at the hospital. My view was that the thinner I was the prettier, better and more sociable I was and therefore the more popular I would be.

I was able to move on from this, but it took time and this included some periods of home schooling – therapy was not an option back then. I certainly did not see my "childbearing hips" or "broad shoulders" as a plus. Interestingly, I never noticed that these hips and shoulders also gave me a great hourglass figure and tiny waist.

Learning to embrace how my body was – to understand that there are things about my body I cannot change – and focusing on being healthy and exercising mind and body, being mindful of my nutrition, has enabled me to love my body shape. I feel my best now actually enhancing the features I once loathed – vintage dresses with tight high waists and pencil skirts are my go-to when I want to feel fabulous. Now I see the benefits of my body and what I have been blessed with. Of course, I have days when I reach for the loose-fitting top (doesn't everyone?) but overall I am happy with my body and have learnt to nurture it for the wonderful role it plays in my life.

Journaling check-in

To keep in mind: Reconnection means authenticity.

How is your journaling going?

What have you learned since completing some of your journal?

What has been difficult and why?

You're doing a great job. Stick with it and let's keep getting reconnected.

The "Wheel of Life"

So far in Part One we have looked at how we see ourselves from a behavioural point of view and from a physical point of view. Now we broaden this out to start to see what's going on in your life as a whole.

A key tool in the coach's box of tricks is the Wheel of Life. It's a mini life audit – allowing you to think about each part of your life and what is happening in each sector. So often we dramatise life: "Everything is awful," "Nothing is going right." When in fact, many parts of our life are doing well and we are content with them.

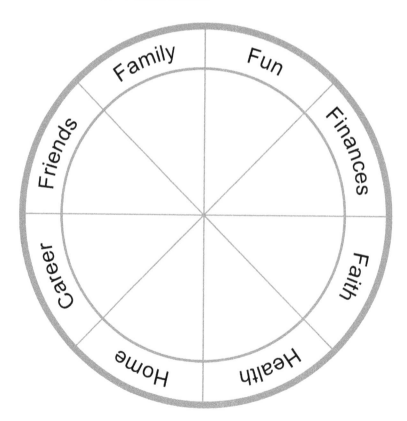

Identifying what parts of our life are in balance helps to stop you going into overwhelm and makes it easier to decide where to put your energy in.

Use the diagram above and score yourself out of 10 for how satisfied you are with these aspects of your life.

What did you notice?

. . . .

. . . .

What is going well in your life?

. . . .

Where do you want to make change?

. . . .

What does change look like?

. . . .

. . . .

It's also interesting as you explore this to think about how the parts of your life play into your values and what is important to you. There can be a clear link between areas of our life which we feel unsatisfied in and how our values are played out in those areas. Are they being valued themselves? Are they being respected?

At the very beginning of the section we looked at areas of your life that were fulfilling or satisfying; how does this link to what you have discovered in the exercises you have done so far in this section?

. . . .

. . . .

How you define yourself

Finally in this section, let's look at how you DEFINE yourself.

We have many labels attributed to us. Labels define us – think about the person who has a career: "I am a lawyer," "I am a teacher," "I am a therapist." It becomes part of our being. It's the same with those roles in life outside of work: "I am a wife, a mother, a daughter…"

As humans, we like to identify those people in our tribes and we are amazing label-creators. Giving something or someone a label gives it a definition and a meaning.

We label cultures, groups, races, gender choices.

It helps us to understand it. Labels can also have powerful effects on our mental health and our behaviour.

In medical terms, many people will have heard the talk about, "Now I know what I am facing, I can begin to fight back," – the person doesn't physically feel any different than they did before the label, but there has been a shift in their thinking.

Or perhaps a label can have the opposite effect. For those diagnosed, for example, with a terminal illness, now they are "a patient that will die" and this can, of course, give a feeling of fear of what will happen in the future.

In my role as a therapist, I often see people owning their own emotions as a label: "I am an anxious/stressed/panicky person..." making it a part of themselves.

Fundamentally, each of these labels gives us a role and in turn creates an image for us, creates a way of seeing ourselves and, as we will soon see in Part Two, creates a way in which others are seen in our lives.

Some roles we choose and hold on to proudly. Some roles we feel are placed upon us.

Use this deconstruction map (another word for mind map) to capture all the roles and labels you have in your life: the generic ones such as relationships and the ones you see yourself as taking on. Really dive down into how many different roles you are playing now. Be really honest and don't think of anything as being too silly to put down. One client put "taxi driver" and "dogsbody" on their map and it helped us to discuss what this meant and it had a real link to a part of the Wheel of Life in which they felt disrespected.

We will come back to this when we look at Reconnection to your universe in Part Three.

Take time to explore how you feel about each of these titles and labels.

What do they mean to you?

....

....

Which do you feel most comfortable with?

....

Which are not sitting in line with your true intentions?

....

A Reconnection moment from me

For me a big Reconnection came at the end of my first full year in business. I was dashing all over the place, saying yes to almost everything and, don't get me wrong, feedback was great and the brand was getting out there. But something wasn't feeling right. I started to become obsessed with the online world of who was doing more – the posts of those who seemed to be getting it all – and I felt I was never keeping up. I was exhausted. I had left a really full-on job that was my life, but on the flipside provided good financial stability for my family, in order to embrace something different. Now I was still exhausted but without the perks and benefits of before. Being a materialistic girl at heart, no matter how connected I am this didn't seem right. I even considered getting another employed role.

I felt as though something wasn't aligned with who I was trying to be – that there was something more, but that it wasn't about bigger and better.

I spent the Christmas break deliberately not working. It was hard to turn my focus away from the business, but I was determined to take my own advice and listen to the silence and see what the message was.

And, of course, it was
STOP–BREATHE–BE PRESENT–BE MINDFUL!

True to form it came through. I realised I needed to focus on what would bring purpose to my life, to *accept* that I was stuck in the "busy", not in the "doing" – this book, the Reconnection programme and the need to study in a whole new direction. I realised if I did this, then the clients and the work would fall into place.

In other words, *purpose* and *intention*.

As I sat and wrote this I was, on the one hand, feeling nervous about changing direction as the business was getting started; but at the same time I was embracing the decision to make this aligned with my purpose – to make life matter.

To round up Part One

Answer the following questions as fully and honestly as possible:

What changes am I making following Part One?

. . . .

. . . .

What "ah-ha" moments did I have?

. . . .

. . . .

How did Part One impact on my emotional wellbeing?

. . . .

. . . .

What did I embrace in my learning?

. . . .

. . . .

Journaling check-in

To keep in mind: Being present is being accepting of now. Reconnection means gratitude for the life that I live.

Before we move on to Part Two, let's check again how your journaling is going?

What have you learned since completing some of your journal?

What has been difficult and why?

You're doing fab. Let's keep reconnecting!

Part Two

RECONNECTING WITH THE WORLD AROUND YOU

This part is all about reconnecting with the wider world around you – looking outside of self and towards how you view your world with others.

Our lives are filled with different people giving us different roles (remember all those roles from Part One). Some we understand and some we are not so sure of. Some individuals we "just get" and others "rub us up the wrong way". Some people stay in our lives for many years and others will come and go within a matter of weeks or months. But every action has a reaction; it has a consequence. It sends a ripple through our universe, via others.

I love the book *The Five People You Meet in Heaven* by Mitch Albom. The lead character, after he has died and gone to Heaven, meets five individuals he has impacted upon. They are not the close friends or relatives he was expecting – some he has not even met in person – but they are the ones on whom he has impacted the most and can learn from the most. The ripples on the surface of his life moved out into their world.

Throughout our lives we have interactions with perhaps hundreds of thousands of people. Every single one of those has an impact – just as in Mitch Albom's book, some will be very visible to us and others will be unseen to us – but they happen. Remember as well that anchor – just as we have an anchor and our chain has a stretch point, so does everyone else!

We cannot avoid having contact with people and all those people have all those things which we explored in Part One: values, things which are important to them, roles and titles, parts of their life they are satisfied and unsatisfied with, their own experiences, dreams and hopes. Each one of those people has something slightly different to us, and yet we are in a world in which we have to have interaction with many different people on a daily basis.

So, gaining an understanding of how those interactions happen and understanding what happens during them for you, and now for the other person, can really help us to move through life together.

Our first port of call is... your support network

These are the people you have around you. Those that you have chosen to be in your tribe or your group. We mentioned in Part One that as humans we look for people to bring into our tribe. We find people that we can rely on, trust and turn to. We might not see at first why they are in our world, so here we explore who you have in your world and perhaps get a different take on what they themselves bring to the table in your world.

In this space list all the people you have in your world (friends, family, work colleagues, acquaintances):

....

....

....

....

What thoughts were coming to mind as you completed this exercise?

....

....

How do you interact with those individuals and what type of support do they give?

....

. . . .

. . . .

Have you ever thought they should give more than what they do?

. . . .

. . . .

Have you ever felt disappointed?

. . . .

. . . .

Often we have a perception or expectation of what people are giving. However, if we stop and think about what their purpose is within their lives and our own, we may see something different.

Client Reconnection story: expectations

Beth had recently started a new business. She was excited and she shared her news with her closest friends. When it came to investing in the business many said they would, but then didn't. Beth felt disappointed in them. She had thought they cared more than this.

But Beth was looking at the world through her own eyes – the business was the most important thing in her life. Her friends really did want her to do well, but life moved on for them. Good intentions and all that.

After chatting it through, Beth reviewed what she gained from them in other ways: the chance to take off her business hat, the chance to be her old self, the ability to gain support when she was feeling tired or frustrated. This was what these people brought to the table. This is what they could give Beth.

- By using the principle of *stop–breathe–be present–be mindful*, Beth could take stock of what was going on right now for her.

- By using the principle of *acceptance*, Beth was able to understand how these individuals fitted in to her world – but also considered what they needed as well.

- By reviewing her *intention* and *purpose*, Beth saw that they brought a lot to the table – just not the investment piece – and could focus her attention on creating external interest in her project.

And so, investment came in from many different angles and all was good – and by looking to see what people could give to her and what they were able to provide (rather than looking to expect what she wanted) Beth was able to redefine her relationships around her.

We explore this concept of roles people play in more depth here in our next exercise.

Expectations and reality – TripAdvisor choice!

If you often feel you have not got what you wanted from those around you and the world, this exercise helps you see how expectations are formed.

Imagine the scene: you are getting ready to choose a holiday. Nowadays we don't really talk to travel agents; we look online and we compare different deals. We get some basic info and some pictures, and we also base our choice often on what other people have said was their own experience. It's like a menu of holidays which you choose from.

The question I ask you, and it's not a trick question, is what is the menu of holidays? Think about what you get on that menu and list it out below.

Menu

. . . .

. . . .

. . . .

Ok, so perhaps you have things like choices, locations, prices, activities, food available and so on.

Now, what happens next?

That's it – you start to narrow it down. You think about where you want to go, what you want included, what type of holiday it is – quiet or active, who is going… You think about where you have already been, discount anything that doesn't meet your needs… You start to create choice.

And you choose! – Fabulous. Now you… book! And you wait to travel…

And in this waiting time, we build on something that has started right at the beginning. We build a picture of what the holiday is going to be. We imagine it, the weather, the room, importantly how it will be and the experience we are going to have. Just like imagining a great meal, we can see it, taste it and smell it!

So, off you go on your travels and you arrive, and my next question – again no tricks here – is what is the holiday?

Holiday

....

....

....

The answer here is actually really simply: The holiday is just that … it's the holiday … it's reality.

The rhetorical question is: Did the holiday match what you ordered? Or more accurately, did the holiday match your expectations of what you ordered?

And you are asking what is this TripAdvisor choice and holidays got to do with relationships? And that answer is… everything!

Remember how you made expectations and assumptions about what you ordered?

The same happens with people in our lives.

Reflect on your interactions with people and how they interact with you.

Are you creating expectations people are not aware of, or perhaps there are expectations on you which you do not wish to fulfil?

Think about that support network you built out. For each of those people, there will be some expectations you have of the individuals involved.

Our parents are a good example of where expectations are sometimes not reality. We have an expectation that our parents will provide love, security, care and comfort. We are shown images of the perfect family where parent and child can have open and honest communication and where the child's needs are met.

For some children this does not happen. There are too many reasons for this to cover in this book (perhaps the next one!) However, what happens is the child grows and will feel disappointment or resentment. It is natural to have these expectations of a parent, but no matter how hard this child wants that to be true, it doesn't happen. The disappointment remains. For whatever reason – perhaps the parent wasn't shown this themselves or they don't know how to be what the child needs or they are distracted by challenges they have themselves – they can't meet the expectations of the child.

In order for the child to start to have a healthier mindset towards this relationship, there needs to be an understanding that reality is not expectation – that what they thought they ordered off the menu of choice they imagined, and it's just not on the menu and it never will be. Now hold your thoughts – this is not about forgiving or simply letting them off the hook; it is simply accepting it is what it is.

Client Reconnection story

Another example of where this happens is with friendships. Joan had been friends with Betty for a few years. Joan classed Betty as a close friend and believed she could trust her. She noticed on occasion that Betty was sometimes indiscreet, but she believed that with their own friendship Betty would not be this way. Betty was fun-loving and outgoing. Always great times were had, and Betty was the first to admit she loved a gossip and was a talker. Joan, however, created an expectation and she "ordered" or chose a friendship assuming trust included discretion.

So although Joan had seen the signs, she shared something private with Betty… and yes of course Betty told someone else, and this led to a real upset for a number of individuals, Joan included.

Joan felt betrayed by Betty – why had she done this to her?

Again, we could say it was natural for Joan to think her friendship would extend to discretion, but let's look back at this.

Betty's friendship role was all about having fun. This was reality. Betty had never said she was the height of discretion. In fact, she had been honest about her weakness for a gossip. Joan had created an expectation that wasn't on the menu and was disappointed when she got served a very different experience… but who created the disappointment in the long term?

So, think about that support network and think about your relationships and perhaps take some time to do a relationship expectation audit on just one or two.

This is a great point to reflect on some of our key steps.

First, *stop–breathe–be present–be mindful*

What is happening in this relationship right now?

. . . .

. . . .

. . . .

What needs does it meet?

. . . .

. . . .

What is causing frustration for me in this relationship?

. . . .

. . . .

What expectations do I have?

. . . .

. . . .

Are these expectations in line with the reality of what they are there to offer?

. . . .

. . . .

Then, let's think about *acceptance*.

If you value the relationship, then there is real need to perhaps change your expectation and accept what they bring to the table in the same way you would like to be accepted.

If you cannot accept their behaviour, then my next section on healthy boundaries and raising your bar will help you put some thought around it.

However, keep this in mind going forward: make careful choice and ensure everyone is clear on what is required on both sides. Don't put in expectations when you choose. Expectation is not communication.

With both the support network and the TripAdvisor choice exercises you are starting to look at your relationships differently. We see people through filters. We see them in our world, based on what we believe to be true.

However, when we step into another's world, only then can we truly see the connection between us.

Imagine this: you meet someone for the first time. You physically see the whole person. But you know only what we know right now about that person – perhaps their name, a potential idea of how they like to dress, their accent so maybe location – and after a few words you have made your impression of them.

And you judge. I say this to all my clients including those in the corporate leadership classes I run: we all judge.

Furthermore, isn't social media – especially Twitter – a clear indicator of that?

In Part One we talked about *acceptance*. This really comes into play here – being accepting of what a person is and that their values are different from yours, accepting what they can and do bring to the table and being accepting of what they can't.

Accept that you can communicate your needs but that some people will never be able to meet them, so then you have always, of course, choice in that relationship.

Let's take a look here at **FORGIVENESS**.

Acceptance and forgiveness are linked. They relate to both you and others, but they are not the same.

Acceptance is exactly that – what has been has been; it cannot be changed. Forgiveness is the ability to let go of that and have a clean slate, so as to speak.

And this is the crucial piece: forgiveness is the right of the wronged! When someone asks for forgiveness, we are brought up to accept their apology and forgive them. It appears to be the right etiquette or part of the rules of life. But forgiveness is not about helping the other person feel better. Forgiveness is all about the person who has been wronged. The ball is in their court; and if this is you, then it is your choice as to whether you wish to forgive. Forgiveness needs to be absolute, not under duress, because if you are not ready then you are not really forgiving – you are just giving in.

You can accept but not forgive and you can forgive but not be accepting. It is my own belief that if you can forgive a person alongside accepting what has happened, it will help you with the healing process, but as a therapist I would never say it is a must and there are for sure things in my life that although I am accepting of, I am not in a place to forgive – and that includes myself.

Take small steps and identify what it really is that needs forgiveness. See how you feel emotionally about this. Think about what will change for the better if you could reach this space.

And my final word on this is that forgiveness does not even need to involve the other person. They may not ask for forgiveness – we have all been there, right? I will forgive them if they ask and apologise, but that might never happen. They may never understand what they did was wrong or may never feel need for forgiveness. So, bring it back to your needs. If you are ready to forgive, then work it through yourself.

Perhaps write a letter you will never send with what you want to say.

Do a ritual where you have that conversation silently.

Meditate or practise mindfulness on the concept of forgiveness.

Then leave it be and move on. Your work is done.

Journaling check-in

To keep in mind: Expectation is not communication. Reconnection means being able to find peace in myself.

Let's check in again on how you are getting on with your journaling. How is it going?

What have you learned since completing some of your journal?

What has been difficult and why?

Onwards and upwards! Let's keep getting reconnected.

Raise your bar – healthy boundaries in relationships

This is one of my favourite lessons in the Reconnection programme. It's also about discussing one of the most frequently considered and most important aspects of client therapy: how much you value yourself but also how you set healthy boundaries for others in your life. Rather than try and split this between Part One on reconnecting with yourself and this part, Part Two on reconnecting with the world around you, I thought it would be a great way to bring it together as our final Part Two exercise.

It's so important that we set standards around behaviours. It's so important that we communicate these standards. A great exercise I use with clients is to visualise a pole vault bar.

Imagine it high up in the air. This is where you need to be in terms of valuing yourself. This is where others need to be when they interact with you, and it's where you want them to be in turn when they think about themselves.

There's space further down for you to create this and really dive into what this means. But before that, let's explore this concept further.

This is NOT about having standards or expectations of self or others which are unreasonable or unobtainable. It *is* about treating yourself with respect and making it clear to others that they need to do the same – because that is how you treat them. It's a cycle of respect and positive communication and relationship.

When you value yourself you treat yourself with kindness. You celebrate your achievements and your skills. You speak kindly to yourself and you don't let negative talk bring you down or prevent you from making progress. You look after yourself physically and mentally.

Others will be able to see this, and you will be able to set your standard for how you are treated by them. Let's take Joan's situation. Joan valued discretion. So when she engaged with friendship with Betty, Joan needed to make that clear. Discretion and no gossip were part of holding Joan's bar high. Not gossiping about Betty was respecting her friendship with Betty and respecting Betty herself.

But Betty didn't get over the bar; she came in underneath the bar. And now Joan has to make a choice. If she values the relationship and can accept what has happened, she needs to talk to Betty about this and discuss how Betty can potentially raise her own bar and not engage in this type of behaviour. But perhaps Betty doesn't want to, and Joan doesn't want to accept. In this case the friendship could end.

BUT – and this is so important – what Joan should never do is simply let it go, simply let Betty think it was OK, because then Betty is always going to come in under the bar. There is no reason to change or aim higher.

And once you start letting people come in under the bar, your bar will get wobbly, it will get lower, you will start to disrespect yourself, and very soon your bar will be on the floor and people will be, as we say, literally walking all over you.

We have all done that, right? I know I have, in all kinds of relationships. I didn't value myself, I didn't expect others to value me, and sometimes I didn't value the other person enough.

Having a clear visual of your bar and where it sits allows you to have boundaries with people and be able to clearly communicate those boundaries with them.

1. Raise your bar high

2. Treat others the same

3. Role model behaviours so they can begin to raise theirs

Client Reconnection story

Ruth came to me following yet another difficult relationship she'd had which had involved violent behaviour and mental abuse. She had a history of picking "the wrong type". Thankfully Ruth had made the call to end the relationship this time and was now seeking support to make change. She wanted to understand why the same thing kept happening.

Ruth had a lot of history from her childhood where she was witness to domestic violence. Her relationship with her mother was very close, but her mother seemed to always need to have a man to "look after her" and yet this would turn controlling and her mother was not able to be strong enough to make change. Ruth didn't get a lot of loving security from her homelife. Praise and self-love were not high on the agenda, and when she grew in to a woman she followed a pattern of seeking out attention from men – looking for someone to "take care of her".

This is just a short summary, of course, of a much more in-depth story. However, what we can now see is that Ruth did not have an understanding of what a high bar meant. She did not value herself because really that had never been displayed to either her or to her mother in a way that was healthy.

Because her bar was pretty low, she accepted behaviour towards her that created a cycle of her trying to be better, feeling it was her fault, and this in turn would lead to further incidents of violence. On the occasions Ruth did walk away, her learnt behaviour and her continued low self-esteem meant she repeated this cycle and wasn't able to communicate boundaries or be confident in how she deserved to be treated.

We spent time (alongside lots of traditional talking therapy to resolve the past traumas) looking at what Ruth brought to the table – how she wanted to be treated, how she could treat herself with kindness, how she could communicate this to others – building her self-esteem and building her confidence. We raised her bar high!

Raise your bar high!

1. Use the space on the following page to draw your bar. Leave space **above it** to write how you believe we deserve to be treated by others.

2. In the space **below the bar** write out behaviours which you do yourself or which others do that now come in under the bar.

3. Finally, make a list of what you would like to change and how this would look going forward.

I deserve to be treated with…

I need to resolve behaviours such as…

I would like to change this to be more…

....

....

Mindfulness moment

This mindfulness exercise can help you to let go of negative aspects of relationships in your life and focus on a more healthy future with good boundaries and expectations in place.

- Use the breathing meditation to gain your focus and mindset.

- Visualise the part of your world you wish to release.

- Slowly imagine you are folding up the image – make it smaller and smaller, folding the picture down firmly so that it is closed.

- When the picture of your image is closed down look and see it become a light feather.

- Watch the feather drift off – taking the image and all negative thoughts with it.

- Breathe out slowly as it rises and visualise the negative energy leaving with it.

Journaling check-in

Let's just check in again on your journaling.

Have you made your connections with three people every day? If not, be committed to this part of the journal in the coming days.

Keep going. You're doing a great job.

Reflection on Part Two

Let's reflect on what we have taken from this time.

What was the "ah-ha" moment that you will remember, and why?

....

....

What have you learned about yourself since you started working through this book?

....

....

What are three changes which you have implemented?

....

....

....

What is the biggest change in you that you perceive or feel?

....

....

Part Three

RECONNECTING WITH YOUR FUTURE DREAMS AND VISIONS

Client Reconnection story

A client of mine had made the move from the big corporate world to set up a service company. He was really keen on this and saw it as his move forward. But it didn't sit comfortably with him. He couldn't embrace it and he kept looking back at his old life, wondering if he had made a mistake.

We did the exercise around labels and titles and how he saw himself, and following this it was clear that his new role was the piece he felt most at odds with. However, it was the thing he wanted to do the most.

We discovered that it wasn't his own judgment of the role that was a problem but the judgment he placed on others – and how he thought they would judge him.

He had been defined by his previous role in the corporate life. He dressed a certain way; he lived a certain life. He saw his new role as a lower role. Albeit it was his own company, it didn't have the same prestige as the one he had left. He presumed others from his previous world would also feel the same way. In this he was judging them badly. He was making assumptions about what they would think of him.

Additionally, he was holding on to that previous life. Self-doubt was causing him to stay locked into the past and worried about his future rather than accepting what was going on. Once he realised this he then had a choice. He could go back to his old life – he was still very much active in there, not wanting to give up things such as his business profile and still following news from his old world – or he could really think about why he decided to leave and what he wanted to do based on his new role in his own company.

That was the Reconnection moment! Once he had made this shift and realised that he had choice and that he actually did want to be in this new life he found it much easier to move on. He stopped comparing himself to where he used to be and realised that actually being his own boss was a status in itself. He embraced the perks of owning your own company and life was much better. Needless to say, his company now started to actually trade and become what he had previously dreamed of.

Bringing it all to the count and to bear!

In Part One we looked at reconnecting with you – understanding what you value and making changes to ensure you are true to those values.

In Part Two we expanded your world to see how you reconnect with those around you. Who is in your support network and what do you expect from people? And is this aligned with what they want and expect to give in terms of support?

Now it is time to really review your own happiness and look to put in place commitments for the ongoing journey.

We are back to where many clients want to start – creating that new world or future place.

But now we have a lot of information under our belt to bring forward, so our thinking can be really critical and we can address where we want to go and how to get there insightfully.

We understand:

1. What's important to us and our values

2. What skills we have and what we bring to the table

3. Who is in our support network and what they bring

4. What we mean by expectations of others versus reality

5. How to set our boundaries and how to have respect for self and others

Using all of this, we can start to really look at that new world. What does it all mean for us? How can we live with intention to meet our purpose?

Remember we spoke about how when we focus on living with intention – being congruent with ourselves and in our relationships – then we create purpose.

The question now is: Has the new world you want to create changed in any way from the one you perhaps imagined when you started on this journey?

Developing resilience and grit

Above all else these two factors are fast becoming the main go-to traits which those that study personality see as key. Many people can start something. Many people can dream and look to achieve; but only a few people will keep moving forward, especially when the terrain is rough.

Resilience is now known to be created during childhood, and again there is so much research and reason for this which we cannot cover in this book, but the main point is it can be built up during adulthood. So, the good news is that even if you have been derailed in the past, you can look to ensure you keep moving forward now. And the positive work on your journal will have been a start to help train your brain to see the world in a different way.

It's really important that you let this sink in – just because you haven't had resilience in the past does not mean it cannot be grown. We used to think that people had a set intelligence, that they could only reach certain levels – now we know that with the right nurturing and environment this can be changed. This is known as "growth mindset" as opposed to "fixed mindset" – work pioneered by another great psychologist Dr Carol Dweck.

The same is true with resilience or grit.

The bestselling writer Dr Paul Stoltz developed the Adversity Quotient or your 'AQ'. This has been measuring how people score in terms of ability to face adversity for some time.

Paul Stoltz's analogy is climbing a mountain

Some individuals will never make a start because climbing the mountain is too hard. These are quitters. Yes, it's not a great word, but it's his word and it describes the behaviour.

Some will get so far and then set up base camp. These are campers.

Some will keep going, reach the peak and move onto the next. In fact, they will actively look for the next peak. These are the climbers. These individuals have a great amount of resilience.

Think about where you are in life right now. (Stop, breathe, be present, be mindful!)

What have you wanted to do but haven't progressed with? Use the following space to make some notes on this.

. . . .

. . . .

. . . .

. . . .

A Reconnection moment from me

Writing this book, I went through all three of these stages!

I had this idea for a book, but I thought: Who would read that? What if I can't do it? How do you even go about writing a book and getting it in print? ... Oh, that looks really hard – there I was a *quitter*!

Thankfully, I had some great advice and I began to think a bit differently. I got some information, I made a start on writing my thoughts down, and I was starting to climb up my mountain, but I still worried about perhaps negative feedback from people and I still didn't have a clue how to create a finished product. So, I set up my base – there I was a *camper*! And I stayed there nice and cosy for quite a long time. I talked around the camp fire of my dreams of writing a book. I told people I was writing a book. I just didn't write it! I joined a whole group of people that are "writing a book".

Finally, after some really good advice and finding some "inner roar" and confidence and working on my writing, I got going again. I guess I must have reached the summit because you're reading it right now! And strangely enough,

I am already now thinking about my next one – the next peak to climb!

Resilience and grit again

A danger that people with goals should watch out for is those around them that have settled where they are and want to draw you in. This is often because they are feeling insecure in their own journey. Some people feel threatened by other people's success. Perhaps on a kinder note they are worried what will happen if you don't achieve (because they are not as focused on achievement as you are, they are trying to protect you based on how they see the world).

Look around you and see who is supporting you in your goals and who seems to be holding you back.

Comments such as, "Oh well, you tried your best," or "It doesn't matter – at least you gave it a go." These are your clues about which group people sit in.

Overall it is resilience which sees us tackle adversity – the ability to face challenges in life and to be able to overcome them rather than see them as a blocker or a reason to stop moving forward.

Grit is the determination which you show to do this. It literally is about sometimes digging deep – like when you join a gym and it's hard and you want to make change but it hurts, but you see how it could be different, you feel dizzy, out of breath, but you focus on the results. You want to step down but find that resilience and you keep going –

just one more minute, 30 more seconds, three more push-ups. You grit your teeth and you dig deep and you make it, and each time you do that you make yourself a little bit better, a little bit stronger, and suddenly a month down the line you notice it feels a bit easier. You don't think you might die right there and then, you have added in something new and different, and you see the difference in yourself!

That's *resilience* and that's *grit* – and it's the opposite of procrastination.

Exercise

Use the table on the opposite page to think out that original question of a goal you wanted to achieve but didn't and see where you might make change and get back on track.

It's important that you be honest with yourself about why you didn't complete it. Think about intention and purpose – think about what's important to you.

Goal I wanted to achieve	
What stopped me?	
What can I do to get restarted?	

Having looked at this and having been honest, here's a concept I want you to really consider now. It's a bit contentious.

What if I just didn't want to do it? – Life 'junk' audit!

How many times have you set yourself a goal… and then never completed it? – like the scrap book of family photos you were going to lovingly build, the crocheting project you were always going to do? For me it's the craft drawers crammed full of bits and bobs for those useful things I am going to make – the Christmas presents that will all be homemade.

Or the course you signed up for… and then didn't really get started.

I'm not talking about the projects you made a great start on then got demotivated slightly and then needed some support. I'm talking about the mythical ones that never really got off the ground, the ones that you quit on before you really made progress.

Why? – what about if you just didn't want to do it!

There I've said it; the cat is out of the bag!

So often we get an idea, or we feel we should be doing something, and we buy all the stuff but then we don't action it. We keep looking at it but never complete it. We come up with lots of excuses like there being no time, but actually we just need to admit: I don't want to do it! I thought I did or I thought I should, but I don't want to do it!"

So now have a think about all the projects you want to do (or think you want to do). List them all down in the first column of the table on the following page, then really think about what they mean to you and about when you plan to do them. When you think about them and actually having to go through with them how do you feel?

Energised or overwhelmed?

Project	Why do I want this? / How does it fit my purpose?	How do I feel about it?

Now really be honest and place all of the projects you have listed into one of the following three categories:

1. I totally want to do this and will set myself a date to complete it by.

2. I want to do this, but I need support, and I will therefore get that support.

3. I don't actually want to do this!

For all those projects you put "1" against, write out a statement with the following form:

I totally want to do this, and I will complete it by [date].

For all those projects you put "2" against, write out a statement with the following form:

I want to do this, but I need support, and I will get this by [activity] or from [person or organisation] and complete the project by [date].

For all those projects you put "3" against, take action now by clearing and decluttering. Empty those craft draws, bag up items that could be used for charities or local groups and in some cases simply throw it out!

I can tell you that you will feel a great weight off your mind. It will free up that virtual space, and I can be certain you will then feel you have time to devote to the projects you really want to focus on.

Client Reconnection story

This client Reconnection story is based on overcoming a challenging belief, but the overall scheme is the same. Ann was feeling stressed and suffering from panic attacks. One of the locations that she worried about most was the large supermarket where she would do the weekly shop. It became a real trigger and she would do anything to avoid it. We worked through her beliefs and where her feelings of panic had come from and she made great progress, yet she still couldn't face the supermarket.

Free from all the baggage of anxiety, we had a Reconnection moment in one session. Ann was able to simply say, "OMG I just really hate supermarkets!" It was such a feeling of relief and she swapped to online shopping and it was job done.

The difference was understanding that she was choosing to not go rather than feeling that she was not going due to fear.

Why resilience is important in this piece

This is because if the reason you don't complete things is not because you don't want to but because you doubt your ability, this could be down to your resilience being low. But remember resilience can be developed and grown.

You can build this by taking one of the projects you do really want to do and then breaking it down into small steps – or stepping stones.

1. List everything out that needs to be done to complete the project.

2. Look at the first thing that needs to happen and break that down even further.

3. Create an action that can be completed within 24 hours of this list being created or even within one hour – such as booking an appointment or ordering some items or clearing space in your diary.

4. Set yourself clear deadlines for when each part is going to be completed and make sure you are clear on what is the outcome or gain that this will give you.

Ticking things off a list gives us a wonderful feeling of achievement. There is an amazing TED talk by Admiral McRaven (Navy Seal) who says that when you get up always make your bed – because that way you have already achieved something and set yourself up for the day.

Every time you complete something tick it off or cross it out and focus on that wonderful feeling of seeing your project move forward.

If moving items around gives you a sense of accomplishment, then you can use the format of the table below to increase this behaviour. I love to use this on a white board with post-it notes because then I can physically move everything around and see progress, but you could also use this format on paper or on screen in whatever way works best for you.

Start with everything in the "To do" column, and as you make a start on items move them to the other columns so you get a clear visual of where you are.

To do (not started)	In progress	Waiting on something	Completed

Your mind map

Ok, so we have now looked at what you want to work on and got rid of excess. You have been thinking about what your future world before this book looked like and whether this has now changed based on understanding more about yourself and your relationships.

Now is time to focus on what the new world will feature.

How I will be

How I will feel

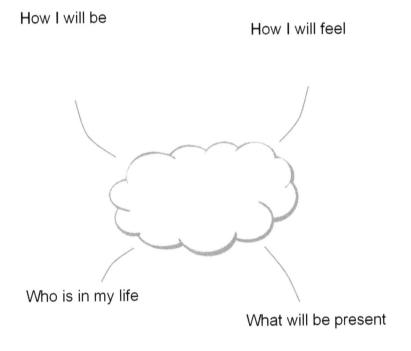

Who is in my life

What will be present

Use the mind map space above to list out everything you would like to be present going forward: your dreams, your aims. You will notice it doesn't just include material things but also focuses heavily on how you will feel and how you will be.

I am a firm believer that when we are congruent in self with how we wish to be, and we feel aligned, then we make progress in the external world.

Write your story

Having gathered all this information together, begin to really see it happening in your mind's eye. Take time to notice all the small details and then put pen to paper and write your story.

This is very different from simply listing out what you want your future to be. This is creating a heart and soul to your future, allowing yourself to see the small details and the fine focus, to be truly in that moment, feeling how you wish to feel, being the person you wish to be and experiencing everything you believe is possible.

Here is an extract of mine.

My days are often varied. I am blessed with having a mixture of tasks throughout my roles. Yesterday I was busy in my therapy room seeing my 1-2-1 clients. It was satisfying to work with them and see them leave after their session with a renewed sense of hope and building upwards for their future. My day finished in time for me to walk to school, the autumn sunshine still creating a warmth to the air and the walk just long enough for me to have time to reflect on my day... before the school door opens and the children pile out. My son sees me and starts to wave, waiting in line impatiently before being released like a horse from the starting gate. He comes flying over and his smile brings me such a feeling of happiness. I decide we shall walk further up to our favourite local café and treat ourselves to cake and myself to a cup of tea.

Today is very different. I am speaking at a very big event on the importance of mental health and the need to stay reconnected. The auditorium seats maybe 200 people and the chairs are raised upwards, so I'm standing on the stage and looking up to the audience able to make eye contact around the room. Although I feel small standing in this space, I feel exhilarated. I love being on stage and public speaking, and it brings me great joy to be able to share my message with others. As I speak I feel myself finding my rhythm and allowing myself to relax into the session, confident in my ability to engage with my audience. Such different daily experiences enable me to stay attuned to my business. (I am such a magpie and distracted by so many new ideas.)

Notice in the extract above how it flows, how it describes the environment, the feelings, how I approach the situation and what the situation brings me. Each part of your future life should be providing nourishment to that purpose and intention, providing a sense of value to the self and allowing you to embrace who you are.

Take time now to build out your story and become familiar with what your new world will look like – because you need to know if you are on track and you need to feel it when you arrive.

Your story

Mindfulness moment – a vision of happiness

Our final exercise is to give you something which will always pinpoint your brain towards a happy place, releasing the required chemicals you need to stay focused and positive.

Doing this exercise helps the brain to get reconnected. Let me explain: when you think of a memory you see the memory and you think only of that memory, but when you think of an object or a word or a phrase you can link this to many memories. Let's work through this below.

Think of a word or a short phrase or an object which conjures up a happy memory.

Don't think of one specific visual memory but of a word, short phrase or object which you associate with a visual memory – for example, I always think of flasks of tea.

Write your word, phrase or the name of your object down.

. . . .

Now picture all the times that word or phrase has been in place for a happy memory. So for me, I have memories of sitting on a beach with my husband, at the park with my nan having a picnic, and going on drives and stopping at the side of the road for a break. You see I have now accessed many different happy memories, creating a greater feeling of happiness overall.

Don't use imaginary scenes. Use real ones, so you really can think about your happy times, your *own* good times, and see them in your mind.

Now when you see the memories brought forward from those initial words or phrases, take more words or phrases that describe them and write those down. Take the words which best describe that scene so you will be able to bring it back when you look and read the words.

Use the space below to write your vision of happiness in words.

. . . .

. . . .

. . . .

And so, we are nearly at the end of our adventure together. By now you will have completed the three parts of the journey – Reconnection with yourself, Reconnection with the world around you and Reconnection with your future dreams and visions. You will also have been filling in your journal for the last 30 days.

It's been a real month of discovery, learning about yourself, being able to try new techniques to create healthy relationships and boundaries, and taking time to focus on where you truly want to go and what you want to put your energy into.

Here are some questions for you to write your answers to.

What have you discovered about you?

. . . .

. . . .

. . . .

What has changed for you in terms of:

1. How you see and treat yourself?

. . . .

. . . .

. . . .

2. How you handle relationships?

. . . .

. . . .

. . . .

3. What your future plans hold?

. . . .

. . . .

. . . .

What has been the biggest "ah-ha" moment for you during this adventure?

. . . .

. . . .

How will you apply this going forward?

. . . .

. . . .

. . . .

Conclusion

KEEPING YOURSELF
RECONNECTED FOREVER

Congratulations, you made it! If you have really committed to completing the exercises in this book and completing the 30 day journal, you will have made some fabulous discoveries and learnt a lot about yourself, the world around you, and your future dreams and visions. So, don't be surprised if you start noticing things a little differently from now on.

Your brain has been undergoing training to be mindful of positive events in your life and you have taken time to really think about what is important to you.

I can't stress enough how wonderful it is that you value yourself enough to have completed this programme and I hope you have enjoyed it.

The key now is to keep focused on where you want to go. If you do nothing else again from the journal, I suggest you keep doing your daily positives, recording all the things that have been positive in your day – firstly because it creates real change in your mindset and secondly because it gives you such a valuable tool to look back on when you are feeling low.

A word of caution! Positive psychology does not mean you feel positive every day – how annoying are those people who are always happy! We as humans are programmed to experience all emotions – none are good or bad in themselves. The trick is to be able to have balance, to see each situation individually and be able to understand that nothing is a permanent state.

What happens if you feel yourself slipping back?

Firstly don't worry – it happens to us all. Think what has brought on these feelings. Think about what you are feeling and what this is trying to tell you.

Perhaps you need to slow down, take stock. You might be tired, overwhelmed; you may need to look at your health and boost yourself.

This is also a great opportunity to review your completed journal – all those positives you collected and all those mindful moments. Pick something from that list and make time to enjoy it.

Find someone to chat to or be self-caring and create some "Me Time" space.

Also, be mindful of what people and places and events have effect on you. Are you spending time with people who are positive in their outlook and lifting you up, or are you getting pulled into negativity and other people's drama? Make some choices and revisit your bar – keep it high!

You might have heard the term "triggers" used. These are things which can bring up those past emotions. Start to be aware of these and understand that the emotions are simply memories of the occasion which has happened.

If in doubt at all, then do seek out professional help. There is no shame or guilt in needing therapy. A healthy mental mindset is something we should all cherish

So, when it rains put up that bright umbrella and your pink wellingtons and enjoy jumping in the puddles. When you truly feel sad be kind to yourself, wrap yourself up, find comfort and allow yourself to feel this, knowing that "it too shall pass!"

Many years ago, when I was in a very dark place, a wise counsellor gave me these words on a card which I have kept ever since, and I leave them with you here as you continue your own path.

It is not because things are difficult we do not try...

it is because we do not try that things are difficult.

You are in investment, you are worthy, and you matter.

Have a wonderful, mindful and happy life ahead.

YOUR
#ReconnectYourLife
30 DAY JOURNAL

These pages should be completed, one a day, as you work through Parts One, Two and Three of the book.

I recommend you do your journaling last thing at night and complete the sections writing by hand. For full instructions and advice on completing the journal pages please see pages 39-42 above. I've included a first page completed with example answers to help you get started.

My positives ++++++

1. Coffee in the sunshine
2. Smooth morning routine
3. ....
4. ....
5. ....
6. ....
7. ....
8. ....
9. ....
10. ....

My top achievement of the day ☆

Found an item I thought was lost

Reconnecting with me!

Yoga routine completed – outdoors!

Mindful moment

Read article in Times on best walks in the UK

Connections I've made 💬

Chatted to the Big Issue Seller

Shared a smile & a laugh with the waitress over breakfast

Said good morning to a stranger whilst walking the dog

My positives ++++++

1. ....
2. ....
3. ....
4. ....
5. ....
6. ....
7. ....
8. ....
9. ....
10. ....

My top achievement of the day ☆

....

Reconnecting with me!

....

Mindful moment

....

Connections I've made 🗨

....

....

....

My positives ++++++

1. ....
2. ....
3. ....
4. ....
5. ....
6. ....
7. ....
8. ....
9. ....
10. ....

My top achievement of the day ☆

....

Reconnecting with me!

....

Mindful moment

....

Connections I've made 💬

....

....

....

My positives ++++++

1. ....
2. ....
3. ....
4. ....
5. ....
6. ....
7. ....
8. ....
9. ....
10. ....

My top achievement of the day ☆

....

Reconnecting with me!

....

Mindful moment

....

Connections I've made 🗨

....

....

....

My positives ++++++

1. ....
2. ....
3. ....
4. ....
5. ....
6. ....
7. ....
8. ....
9. ....
10. ....

My top achievement of the day ☆

....

Reconnecting with me!

....

Mindful moment

....

Connections I've made ⬤

....

....

....

My positives ++++++

1. ....
2. ....
3. ....
4. ....
5. ....
6. ....
7. ....
8. ....
9. ....
10. ....

My top achievement of the day ☆

....

Reconnecting with me!

....

Mindful moment

....

Connections I've made ♡

....

....

....

My positives ++++++

1. ....
2. ....
3. ....
4. ....
5. ....
6. ....
7. ....
8. ....
9. ....
10. ....

My top achievement of the day ☆

....

Reconnecting with me!

....

Mindful moment

....

Connections I've made ⤴

....

....

....

My positives ++++++

1. ....
2. ....
3. ....
4. ....
5. ....
6. ....
7. ....
8. ....
9. ....
10. ....

My top achievement of the day ☆

....

Reconnecting with me!

....

Mindful moment

....

Connections I've made 💬

....

....

....

My positives ++++++

1. ....
2. ....
3. ....
4. ....
5. ....
6. ....
7. ....
8. ....
9. ....
10. ....

My top achievement of the day ☆

....

Reconnecting with me!

....

Mindful moment

....

Connections I've made ⏹

....

....

....

134

My positives ++++++

1. ....
2. ....
3. ....
4. ....
5. ....
6. ....
7. ....
8. ....
9. ....
10. ....

My top achievement of the day ☆

....

Reconnecting with me!

....

Mindful moment

....

Connections I've made 💬

....

....

....

NO ONE CAN MAKE YOU FEEL OR THINK WHAT
YOU CHOOSE NOT TO.

My positives ++++++

1. ....
2. ....
3. ....
4. ....
5. ....
6. ....
7. ....
8. ....
9. ....
10. ....

My top achievement of the day ☆

....

Reconnecting with me!

....

Mindful moment

....

Connections I've made 💬

....

....

....

My positives ++++++

1. ....
2. ....
3. ....
4. ....
5. ....
6. ....
7. ....
8. ....
9. ....
10. ....

My top achievement of the day ☆

....

Reconnecting with me!

....

Mindful moment

....

Connections I've made ♡

....

....

....

My positives ++++++

1. ....
2. ....
3. ....
4. ....
5. ....
6. ....
7. ....
8. ....
9. ....
10. ....

My top achievement of the day ☆

....

Reconnecting with me!

....

Mindful moment

....

Connections I've made 💬

....

....

....

My positives ++++++

1. ....
2. ....
3. ....
4. ....
5. ....
6. ....
7. ....
8. ....
9. ....
10. ....

My top achievement of the day ☆

....

Reconnecting with me!

....

Mindful moment

....

Connections I've made 🗩

....

....

....

My positives ++++++

1. ....
2. ....
3. ....
4. ....
5. ....
6. ....
7. ....
8. ....
9. ....
10. ....

My top achievement of the day ☆

....

Reconnecting with me!

....

Mindful moment

....

Connections I've made 🗩

....

....

....

My positives ++++++

1. ....
2. ....
3. ....
4. ....
5. ....
6. ....
7. ....
8. ....
9. ....
10. ....

My top achievement of the day ☆

....

Reconnecting with me!

....

Mindful moment

....

Connections I've made 💬

....

....

....

EXPECTATIONS ARE NOT THE SAME AS COMMUNICATION.

My positives ++++++

day
16

1. ....
2. ....
3. ....
4. ....
5. ....
6. ....
7. ....
8. ....
9. ....
10. ....

My top achievement of the day ☆

....

Reconnecting with me!

....

Mindful moment

....

Connections I've made 💬

....

....

....

My positives ++++++

1. ....
2. ....
3. ....
4. ....
5. ....
6. ....
7. ....
8. ....
9. ....
10. ....

My top achievement of the day ☆

....

Reconnecting with me!

....

Mindful moment

....

Connections I've made 🗩

....

....

....

My positives ++++++

1. ....
2. ....
3. ....
4. ....
5. ....
6. ....
7. ....
8. ....
9. ....
10. ....

My top achievement of the day ☆

....

Reconnecting with me!

....

Mindful moment

....

Connections I've made 🗩

....

....

....

My positives ++++++

1. ....
2. ....
3. ....
4. ....
5. ....
6. ....
7. ....
8. ....
9. ....
10. ....

My top achievement of the day ☆

....

Reconnecting with me!

....

Mindful moment

....

Connections I've made 🗩

....

....

....

145

My positives ++++++

1. ....
2. ....
3. ....
4. ....
5. ....
6. ....
7. ....
8. ....
9. ....
10. ....

My top achievement of the day ☆

....

Reconnecting with me!

....

Mindful moment

....

Connections I've made 🗩

....

....

....

My positives ++++++

1. ....
2. ....
3. ....
4. ....
5. ....
6. ....
7. ....
8. ....
9. ....
10. ....

My top achievement of the day ☆

....

Reconnecting with me!

....

Mindful moment

....

Connections I've made 💬

....

....

....

My positives ++++++

1. ....
2. ....
3. ....
4. ....
5. ....
6. ....
7. ....
8. ....
9. ....
10. ....

My top achievement of the day ☆

....

Reconnecting with me!

....

Mindful moment

....

Connections I've made 💬

....

....

....

My positives ++++++

1. ....
2. ....
3. ....
4. ....
5. ....
6. ....
7. ....
8. ....
9. ....
10. ....

My top achievement of the day ☆

....

Reconnecting with me!

....

Mindful moment

....

Connections I've made 💬

....

....

....

My positives ++++++

day
24

1. ....
2. ....
3. ....
4. ....
5. ....
6. ....
7. ....
8. ....
9. ....
10. ....

My top achievement of the day ☆

....

Reconnecting with me!

....

Mindful moment

....

Connections I've made 💬

....

....

....

My positives ++++++

1. ....
2. ....
3. ....
4. ....
5. ....
6. ....
7. ....
8. ....
9. ....
10. ....

My top achievement of the day ☆

....

Reconnecting with me!

....

Mindful moment

....

Connections I've made 🗩

....

....

....

My positives ++++++

1. ....
2. ....
3. ....
4. ....
5. ....
6. ....
7. ....
8. ....
9. ....
10. ....

My top achievement of the day ☆

....

Reconnecting with me!

....

Mindful moment

....

Connections I've made 💬

....

....

....

IT'S NOT ABOUT HOW LOUD YOU SHOUT...
IT'S ABOUT HOW CLEAR YOU ROAR!

My positives ++++++

day
27

1. ....
2. ....
3. ....
4. ....
5. ....
6. ....
7. ....
8. ....
9. ....
10. ....

My top achievement of the day ☆

....

Reconnecting with me!

....

Mindful moment

....

Connections I've made 💬

....

....

....

My positives ++++++

1. ....
2. ....
3. ....
4. ....
5. ....
6. ....
7. ....
8. ....
9. ....
10. ....

My top achievement of the day ☆

....

Reconnecting with me!

....

Mindful moment

....

Connections I've made ⬭

....

....

....

My positives ++++++

1. ....
2. ....
3. ....
4. ....
5. ....
6. ....
7. ....
8. ....
9. ....
10. ....

My top achievement of the day ☆

....

Reconnecting with me!

....

Mindful moment

....

Connections I've made 🗩

....

....

....

DON'T BE AFRAID TO SET UP YOUR BOUNDARIES... VALUE YOURSELF,
VALUE OTHERS... TEACH THEM TO DO THE SAME.

My positives ++++++

1. ....
2. ....
3. ....
4. ....
5. ....
6. ....
7. ....
8. ....
9. ....
10. ....

My top achievement of the day ☆

....

Reconnecting with me!

....

Mindful moment

....

Connections I've made 🗩

....

....

....

Recommended reading

I recommend the following books as further reading:

Thrive – Arianna Huffington

The Seat of the Soul – Gary Zukav

Trust – Iyanla Vanzant

Mindset – Dr Carol Dweck

The Chimp Paradox – Prof Steve Peters

The Five People You Meet in Heaven – Mitch Albom

What I Know for Sure – Oprah Winfrey

Inspirational Fabulous and Over 40! – Clare Cahill and Jo Outram (Eds.)
This is a collection of the stories from women who have turned their life around from 40 onwards. I'm one of the contributing authors.

Lightning Source UK Ltd.
Milton Keynes UK
UKHW020657110321
380169UK00012B/875